THE
CHILEAN
KITCHEN

Skyhorse Publishing books may be purchased in bulk at special discounts for sales promotion, corporate gifts, fund-raising, or educational purposes. Special editions can also be created to specifications. For details, contact the Special Sales Department, Skyhorse Publishing, 307 West 36th Street, 11th Floor, New York, NY 10018 or info@skyhorsepublishing.com.

Skyhorse® and Skyhorse Publishing® are registered trademarks of Skyhorse Publishing, Inc.®, a Delaware corporation.

Visit our website at www.skyhorsepublishing.com.

10 9 8 7 6 5 4 3 2

Library of Congress Cataloging-in-Publication Data is available on file.

Cover and interior design by Daniel Brount
Cover photo by Araceli Paz

Print ISBN: 978-1-5107-5285-6
Ebook ISBN: 978-1-5107-5286-3

Printed in China

THE
CHILEAN
KITCHEN

75 Seasonal Recipes for Stews, Breads, Salads, Cocktails, Desserts, and More

Pilar Hernandez and Eileen Smith

Photography by Araceli Paz

Skyhorse Publishing

Contents

Introduction

Travel anywhere in the world, and people will ask you about your country's most traditional food. Continue on, and they might ask about your dance, your flag, or your flower. In Chile the answers to most of these questions is simple. The dance? The *cueca*, a coquettish coupled folk dance, where dancers hold and twirl white kerchiefs. The flag? Not dissimilar to that of Texas, red, white, and blue, with a lone white star on a blue background in the upper left corner. Our flower is the *copihue*, or Chilean bellflower, a waxy pinkish bloom that hangs from a climbing vine that prefers the Valdivian rainforest in the mid-south of Chile.

But what about our food? You might know Chile best for wine, or maybe the bulk of your fruit that comes in the off-season—berries, and apples, and maybe avocado, depending on where you live. But these products tell the tiniest sliver of the story. There is no simple answer to describe our food, but this book is a good start. Reading it and preparing these meals will give you a better understanding of Chile's dishes, history, culture, and language, and how they are

all braided together to give us what we call *comida chilena* (Chilean food).

Chilean food traces its roots through our history, from indigenous cultures, pre-Columbian settlements, Spanish colonization, and waves of immigration since then. In the larger context of Latin American food, it can be described as *criolla*, a word used to mean the mix of Spanish and indigenous influences. But in day-to-day life, most people don't choose to use the word *criolla*, and instead call it *comida chilena*.

Though we can more or less agree on what to call it, it's important to point out that what is considered traditional is a bit of a moving target. Some of the dishes we consider to be most Chilean, and which even Oreste Plath, one of Chile's most well-known folklorists and food historians, wrote about as early as the 1960s, trace back their roots to Germany, France, Peru, and Italy. And yet, our concept of Chilean food evolves, and it doesn't take long for new foods to become new "Chilean favorites." We have only to look at the popularity of desserts with blueberries in the south of Chile to see this. It may feel like we've eaten them forever, but blueberries were not cultivated here until the 1980s.

Chilean cuisine has been in a huge state of flux in recent decades. The introduction of new agricultural products is likely to continue to change the face of Chilean food, as will other global influences. Chileans who travel or live abroad and then come back to visit will introduce innovation, and importantly, the influx of people from other countries, such as the recent arrival of many Venezuelans and Haitians to Chile, will change the face of Chilean food.

Talking about what Chilean food is today requires a little bit of historical context. Chile was poor for much of its history, and the social climate during the dictatorship from 1973 to 1990 did not allow restaurant culture to proliferate in Chile as it did in Europe or North America during that period. Another defining feature of Chilean food is the country's geography. Chile is only about 220 miles wide at its widest point, yet extends more than 2,600 miles along the Pacific coast. If you were to fold a world map in half at the equator, and superimpose Chile onto the northern hemisphere, Chile would extend from Alaska to Guatemala. Regional cooking styles have not mixed much from north to south due to great distance and the differing availability of products in each region. The long distance and historical lack of good infrastructure to move products around means we all tend to favor products that are locally and seasonally available.

What we present here in *The Chilean Kitchen* is a snapshot of *comida chilena* that you could find in Chilean kitchens from approximately the 1980s through today. It is the food we seek out in restaurants and cook at home. It is the food of grandparents and weekends in the country, of comfort food and *así un plato* (a serving *thiiiis* big).

Many of the recipes in this book are from the central region of Chile, where nearly half of the country's 18 million residents live. There is a common refrain here, which is *Santiago no es Chile* (Santiago is not Chile). And we know this is true. But for practical reasons, we had to limit the scope of this book, even as we wish we'd had the space to more fully explore the cuisines of the far north, with its minty *rica-rica* and llama stews, or the lamb-rich culture of the far south and its delectable *murta*, *murtilla*, and *calafate* berries. We'd love to dedicate time to the island cuisines of Chile, their *seriola* (amberjack), crab, lobster, and sea snails that are seldom seen in central Chile. We have much love for these regional specialties and other favorites that did not make it into this book. We hope to continue exploring and writing about all of these, and so much more, at a later date.

We are so excited for you to use this book to learn about the homey, timeless classics of Chile, those to which we gravitate when the very best ingredients are in season. We are a culture of stews. Of squash and corn and tomatoes. Of meat (but not that much) and salads, so many salads. Of bread. Of celebrating with desserts and empanadas and *completos* (Chilean-style hot dogs).

Chilean food is not spicy. It is comforting and easily identifiable, with no hidden ingredients. We lean on the barely sweet flavors of cooked onions and oregano, and liven up winter dishes with cumin or a nice *sofrito* with red bell peppers. Nearly all of the ingredients we cook with will be familiar to you, but the combinations make all the difference, as you will soon see.

When possible, we source our food close to home. For fruit and vegetables, if we don't have our own *chacra* (vegetable garden), we choose *ferias*, or farmers' markets, following calls of "*casera, caserita*" (something like: valued customer) to the stands we know and love, featuring locally grown fruit and vegetables. Maybe a vendor will tempt you to buy his fruit, by calling out a price, "*a mil a mil a mil las frutillas*" (strawberries for 1,000 pesos), or naming the dishes you might make with their products, saying "*ricas las cebollas, para la cazuela, para las empanadas, para la ensalada chilena*" (delicious onions, for soup, for empanadas, for Chilean salad).

Once our carts or bags are full, we head home, which is where it all unfolds. Chilean cooking takes place indoors and outdoors, on stove tops in urban apartments, on wood-burning stoves in the far south, or, where we have the luxury, outside in a separate area with a barbecue, clay oven, or a type of grill made from a metal drum.

Ovens are mainly reserved for baking cakes and other desserts, because using a gas oven is more expensive than cooking on the stove top. Also, most of Chile uses propane tanks, delivered by truck or cargo tricycle, to fuel the stove, so we're always mindful of the possibility of running out of gas. Soups and stews can be turned off and on again without suffering in quality, but a fallen cake is not so easily disguised.

Cooking and eating and home are central parts of Chilean community and family life. Wander through the kitchen and you might be given a preview snack, or be asked to shell beans into a metal bowl. Long, after-meal conversations at the dining room table are such an integral part of our culture that we have a special word for it, the *sobremesa*.

Our food, language, and culture are so interwoven that even our language is peppered with food-related expressions. We have e*n todas partes se cuecen habas* (literally, "people cook fava beans all over the world"), meaning that bad things happen everywhere. And there is one of many Chilean expressions meaning that someone is getting on your last nerve, which is *me sacaron los choros del canasto* (literally, "they took mussels out of my basket").

This book of Chilean recipes is about so much more than just the foods we eat. It is an invitation to understand Chilean culture. For each dish, we have looked at the historical, linguistic, and cultural roots and written about what it means to Chileans. We have relied on dozens of years of our own experiences and countless conversations with the larger Chilean community both in person and through Pilar's sizeable online community.

Pilar, who wrote the recipes, grew up surrounded by fearless home cooks in Rancagua, a small Chilean city, and also on the coast at her grandparents' home. Life and work took her to Houston, Texas, in 2003, far away, for the first time, from her extended Chilean community. She turned to re-creating Chilean cuisine in the United States and started what is now one of the most well-known blogs from Chile (*En Mi Cocina Hoy*), which now has a sister site in English called *Chilean Food and Garden*. However, through the community engagement that formed around her blog, Pilar soon found that she is not alone in wanting to cook *comida chilena*. It has become an invaluable resource for people who—for reasons of time or distance—find themselves without access to these elemental foods of their own Chilean identity.

Pilar's experiences throughout childhood of visiting and eating meals with people of every stripe in nearby communities taught her the value of being a good listener and member of the community. She remembers her family homes as inclusive places where everyone was always welcome. She attributes her own spirit of generosity to how she is raised, and hopes to pass it along to her own children as well.

With her blog, Pilar has also contributed to the canon of Chilean cookery. She started with traditional recipes that serve up to twenty, and winnowed them down and reinvented them to be suitable for modern households and kitchens. Her methodical, scientific approach to recipe development and testing (after all, she is trained as a physician) have helped her develop a significant body of reliable recipes, imbued with the spirit of the community in which she was raised. The blog has allowed Pilar to keep a strong connection with Chile as well as establishing her as part of a community of Latina bloggers in the United States, which she also relishes.

For good or bad, many Chileans have a tendency to overvalue things from outside of the country and undervalue things that are homegrown. In that sense, you could say Pilar is a bit of a maverick when it comes to Chilean cooking. She is notoriously food-trend-averse and stands by these recipes that will last for generations, long after the fascination with kombucha or grain-free cooking have passed out of fashion.

Eileen, who wrote the text for the book, is originally from Brooklyn, New York, but has lived on the east and west coasts of the United States, never more than a few hours from the ocean. Before moving to Chile in 2004, she spent time in several Spanish-speaking countries, and came to Chile in part to help solidify her Spanish. She is trained as a lawyer and worked as a journalist before coming to Chile. Eileen writes about the things that make us human, including food, drink, culture, travel, design, and language. She writes for different websites, companies, guidebooks, apps, and magazines in addition to writing on her own website, bearshapedsphere.com.

When she moved to Chile, Eileen found herself routinely trying to re-create the home cooking of her Ashkenazi Jewish childhood, often traversing wide swaths of Santiago by bike to pick up hard-to-find ingredients. Over time, her favorites expanded to include newer dishes, and the day she first tasted Chilean *porotos granados* (Bean, Corn, and Squash Potage, see page 29), she knew she had found a new comfort food.

Eileen is very interested in memoir and how we experience nostalgia on a daily basis. After reading many lackluster reports of Chilean food that she felt failed to capture the context, history, and importance of Chilean cuisine to the culture, she decided to throw her hat in the ring. She soon realized that she could also help tell the story of Chilean food, not just through her own observations, but by helping to provide a signal boost to the voices of Chileans involved in food. She started interviewing people in the food and wine industry, using her own observations to shape the questions and using her connections in publishing to showcase other people's stories.

Pilar and Eileen met in the most modern of ways—through social media, each having read the other's blog sometime in the late 2000s. Some years later, Eileen pitched an article to NPR's *The Salt* about the *marraqueta*, a type of bread popular in central Chile. She hoped to write a piece that Chileans would identify with and to imbue the piece with the attachment that Chileans have to their own cuisine and traditions, and she interviewed Pilar for the piece. A couple of years later, Pilar approached Eileen to work together on an idea she'd been brewing: writing this cookbook of recipes and stories of the Chilean kitchen that would one day make it into your hands.

Together we have collaborated on *The Chilean Kitchen* over a period of nearly two years. We have spoken about our experiences in Chile, in the United States, about foods, traditions, nostalgia, similarities and differences, misunderstandings and mischaracterizations of our home cultures in our new, adopted ones, and about all the things that make food taste like home.

When we signed the book contract, we already had a photographer in mind. Araceli Paz is a talented Chilean food photographer, visual artist, and adventurer, and we knew she would know as much about and be just as passionate about Chilean food as we are. We flew in from far corners of the globe and worked together for a solid ten days in Pilar's kitchen in Houston. There, we cooked, styled, shot, talked about, reminisced, wrote about, and enjoyed seventy-five recipes' worth of food and drink in short order. Every evening we packed out huge takeaway containers to nearby Chilean friends and family. Later at night, we reread the recipes and texts, making changes so that we could bring you the truest iterations of these stories and recipes.

The Chilean Kitchen is our love letter to the food of a country that has molded who we are today. We are so excited for you to cook these traditional recipes, to fill your kitchens with the enticing smells and warmth, and share Chilean food with your own communities, new and old. We can't wait to hear how it goes.

Chilean Pantry

Most of the ingredients and utensils you will need for the recipes in this cookbook you will already have in your kitchen. A few "essentials" are listed below. First, we've listed Chilean ingredients that are commonly found in the United States, followed by lesser-known ones. Then we talk about the kitchen implements that no Chilean kitchen would be without.

COMMON CHILEAN INGREDIENTS

Aceitunas de Azapa: These Chilean olives come from the Azapa Valley, in the north of Chile. They are purple in color, and have a less dense flesh, but a similar bite to kalamata olives. *Aceitunas de Azapa* have a denomination of origin.

Ají cacho de cabra: A red pepper called "goat's horn pepper" in English that is mainly used dried. Substitute cayenne pepper.

Ají verde/cristal: This is a mild-to-medium pepper that is used from green to red. It is about four inches long. We use it raw in salads and sometimes cooked. A good replacement available in the United States is a sweet banana pepper or yellow Thai pepper.

Blue eggs: These come from the Araucana chicken, a breed that comes from the Araucanía Region in the mid-south of Chile. We see these commonly even in Santiago, but they are considered a specialty item, as most eggs in Chile are white or brown.

Camarón de barro: These are crawfish, which are dug from beside rivers, and are a regional specialty. We include them as an option in *Chupe de Mariscos*/Baked Seafood Casserole (page 95).

Chilean corn: The corn we use in Chile is starchy and much larger than the corn on the cob you might be familiar with in the United States, being more similar to the corn used to make *pozole* in Mexican cooking.

Chilean mustard: The prepared mustard we eat in Chile is much sweeter and less tangy than the mustard people generally eat in the United States.

Chilean Pisco: In Chile, pisco has a denomination of origin, and may only be produced in certain regions in the near north of the country, and with certain grapes. Look for smaller production for more flavorful, fruity Chilean piscos, as many of the mass-market ones tend to be milder in flavor.

Color: This seasoning is made by melting pork fat and adding sweet paprika to it. At room temperature, it is solid, and it can be used to start a *sofrito*, and in some cases, scooped on top of soups. It adds a warm color and a mild flavor.

Cornmeal: We use cornmeal in Chile primarily to thicken soups and stews. Traditional Chilean cornmeal, called *chuchoca*, is cooked and dried in the sun in artisanal production. Do not substitute polenta or grits, which, though also dried, are coarser and uncooked.

Longaniza: When we talk about *longaniza* in Chile, we are talking about an artisanal pork sausage in a beef casing. Normally they would be made in butcher shops, where they are hung to dry. The mid-southern city of Chillán is considered to be the capital of this type of sausage, and it is common for travelers to bring it back to their hometowns when passing through that city.

Merkén: A smoky pepper powder made of *ají cacho de cabra* (see above) and sometimes cilantro seeds and salt. It comes to us from the indigenous Mapuche people and is first dried in the sun, and then smoked over a wood fire. It is used as a rub, and in soups, and some people sprinkle it on sandwiches or stews.

Miel de palma: Chilean palm syrup. A dark caramel-colored syrup made from boiling the sap of the Chilean palm tree. It is easily replaced with palm syrup or coconut nectar you can find in the United States.

Miel de ulmo: In Chile, we distinguish among the many different types of honey, and this one, made by bees that gather nectar from blooms of the *ulmo* (Eucryphia cordifolia) tree, is especially prized.

Mote: This is the peeled and cooked wheat kernel that we use in Chile in savory dishes and one dessert (*Mote con Huesillos*/Sweetened Dried Peach Punch with Barley, see page 131). As it can be difficult to source in the United States, we have substituted barley with very similar results.

Pasta de ají: A vinegar and hot pepper condiment that is thicker than Tabasco but smoother than salsa. It is often purchased commercially, and may be added to *pebre* or other sauces or put on empanadas.

Quinoa: The ancient grain of the Inca, which is high in protein and traditionally eaten in the north of Chile. It has become more popular all over Chile in recent years and is often presented as part of a risotto-like dish.

Sea salt from Cahuil: This is another product that has a denomination of origin in Chile, It dissolves easily, and contains magnesium and other trace elements. It is preferred by many home cooks and restaurant chefs.

Vegetable oil: In Chile we commonly use vegetable oil, not olive oil, especially for cooking. Sunflower oil or grapeseed oil are commonly used, though this may vary by household.

HARDER TO SOURCE CHILEAN INGREDIENTS

We hope that in using this book, you will be inspired to learn more about Chilean food. If you continue your research, you will come across some ingredients and preparations that we did not include because they are not easily available in the Untied States. Below we have listed some that represent the north, south, middle, and island territories of Chile. Because you are unlikely to be able to track down these products locally, you might just have to come for a visit and try these delicacies straight from the source.

Starting with products that grow aboveground, we include here a variety of lemon from an oasis in the north, called *limón de pica*, the *piñon*, a large pine nut from the *araucaria* (monkey puzzle tree), *nalca*, which is the crunchy stem of a giant-leaved plant which resembles (but is unrelated to) rhubarb, the *chagual*, a vegetable product that's part of a giant bromeliad flower, the *avellana chilena*, also known as the Chilean hazelnut, which is actually the seed of an evergreen tree, and *penca*, often translated as cardoons, a type of edible thistle.

Moving on to items that grow underground, we're big fans of *ajo chilote*, a huge type of garlic grown on the island of Chiloé that is similar to elephant garlic. Also native to Chiloé, the ancestral home to many potatoes are the *papas chilotas*, several varieties of knobby potatoes that come in many colors including an eye-catching purple.

From the ocean, there is a plethora of seafood that is well known in Chile including *piures* (red sea squirts), *locos* (Chilean abalone) specialty lobsters from the Juan Fernandez islands and Easter island, *picorocos* (giant barnacles), *centolla* (king crab), and *lapas* (limpets). Not to be outdone by the seafood, we also have two parts of the same giant bull kelp (*Durvillaea antarctica*) which are commonly eaten in Chile, *cochayuyo*, which is the long tentacle-like part, used in soups, stews, salads, and empanadas, as well as given dried to children to teethe on, and the anchor of the same seaweed, *ulte* which is sometimes used in *pebre*.

After these cultivated products are a few items that take a human touch to create. These include *chicha*, a type of cider made from apples or grapes depending on the region, *harina tostada*, a toasted flour sprinkled on watermelon or mixed with hot water to make a porridge eaten for breakfast or a snack, and *charqui*, which is a simple jerky of salted dried meat without additional flavorings. In Chile, this is most commonly made from horse or llama meat. *Aliño completo*, a dried flavoring mix, may be called for in some recipes, but we prefer to doctor our recipes to taste, using cumin, oregano, and onions separately. *Motemei* is a type of hominy-like corn prepared as we would prepare pearled barley or *mote* (peeled wheatberries), and is the starchy backbone of many specialty savory dishes.

KITCHEN EQUIPMENT

Box grater: For Chilean food you mainly only need the coarse side, and no well-equipped Chilean kitchen would ever be without a box grater. It is most commonly used to grate carrots or occasionally beets.

Chilean toaster: This square grill sits atop a gas burner to muffle the flame under rice, or to toast bread or empanadas. Similar ones are in use in Japan and Italy, and they are frequently brought home as souvenirs or gifts for other cooks from Chile.

Citrus juicer: While some people may have a press, in most traditional Chilean homes, this will be the kind of plastic juicer that sits on a table or counter and is used to make fresh-squeezed lemon juice.

Green bean slicer: This small kitchen gadget, which is about the size of a vegetable peeler, is used to French cut green beans. You push the green bean through on one side and it is sliced by a crosshatch of wires into narrow slices. In the United States, it's easier to purchase French-cut frozen green beans.

Individual-sized double-handled frying pan: In Chile this *paila* is used from stove to table for serving individual portions of scrambled eggs, and most Chilean homes would have a set, though you can work around it if you don't.

Knives: To prepare the food in this cookbook, you will not need a large variety of knives. We suggest one serrated knife for cutting bread and tomatoes, one paring knife for smaller jobs and peeling (though you can use a vegetable peeler if you prefer), and one chef's knife.

Salt jar: We keep a jar of salt in the kitchen for cooking, often with a spoon in it. This has confused more than one traveler who has inadvertently tipped a spoonful of salt into their tea.

Small mesh colander: Practical for straining out lemon seeds, dusting pastries with powdered sugar, or fishing out dumplings from soup before putting it in the fridge.

Teakettle: Two main versions of this exist in the Chilean kitchen, the electric teakettle, which is popular because it turns off automatically, and the *pava*, or metal teakettle that sits on the stove.

Twine: We use this to tie bundles of herbs for soups and stews, and for *humitas*, which are our version of tamales, made with fresh corn.

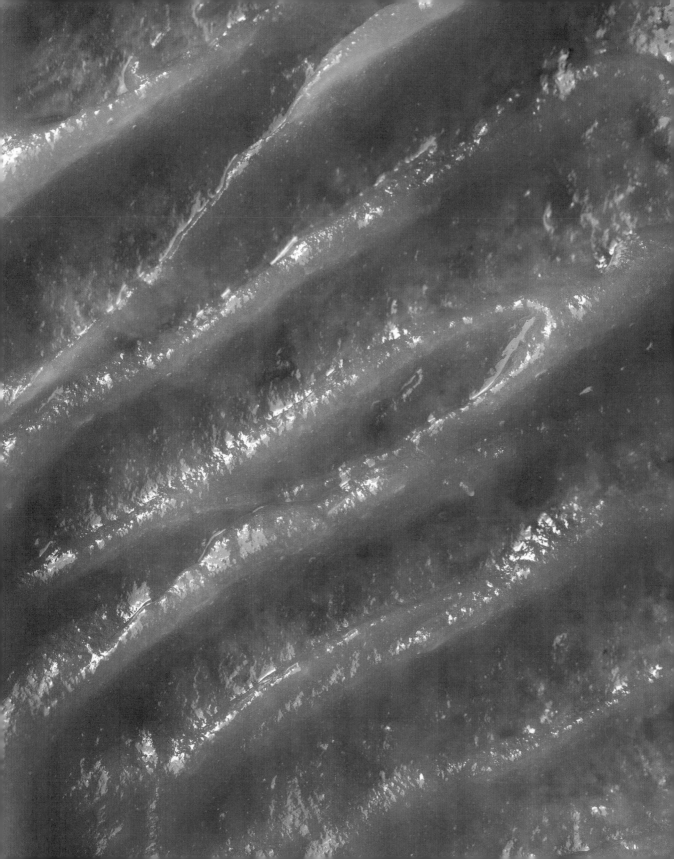

Summer

Summer in Chile, those delicious months between December and March, starts with a boom, with the end of the academic year and Christmas and then New Year's piling one on top of the other. After that frenetic energy ebbs, the days stretch long and languid as many families pack up and head out of town. Most people in Chile take at least a couple of weeks off in January or February, and head to wherever their history and budget take them.

One of the most important parts of the summer getaway, whether to the beach or a lake, is the route you take to get there. Black signs with white numbers dot the roadside, advertising tomatoes by the crateful or giant bunches of basil, their roots still attached. These we pick up as we make the leisurely drive to our destination. The vegetables lend their perfume to the drive, with promises of salads and other simple summery dishes, as watermelons roll around in kids' foot space.

Once we get to the beach, cabin, or country, we unpack and settle in, ready to spend lazy afternoons with extended family, often headed by grandparents who run the ship while parents work in the city and come out on weekends. Summer in Chile is the very embodiment of "it takes a village," a multigenerational mix of adults and kids with an ever-rotating cast.

Summer is a convivial season, with free time, relaxed bedtimes, and plenty of dessert and celebration and fresh air. In summer, it's easy to feel like we're soaking up the essence of unstructured time and sunshine to last us the whole year round. On our drive back to the city at the end of vacation, we'll pick up a flat of the last farmstand peaches and other fresh-from-the-soil treats to bring a touch of summertime back to the city with us.

Summer

MELÓN CON VINO

White Wine Sipped from a Honeydew

SERVES 4

Think of melón con vino as an inside-out sangria that comes in its own vessel. Take a honeydew, cut and scoop it like a jack-o-lantern (please forgo the eye and mouth holes), and pour in white wine. It's an out-doorsy, picnic-and-barbecue-friendly drink that you can assemble in situ, with nothing more than chilled melons, sugar, wine, a knife, a spoon, and a straw.

If you're thinking a melon full of wine seems like a lot of wine for one person to drink, it is. People usually drink melón con vino communally with multiple straws, and keep pouring in wine until there's none left, or someone decides they want a snack and starts eating the melon innards. Young people in Chile today often refer to it as "melvin," a portmanteau made of the first syllables of each of the Spanish words, melón and vino. It's popular among the college set, or among recent grads. From a distance, it looks a bit like you're drinking coconut water out of a green coconut, but we don't recommend using a machete.

1 cold honeydew melon
½ cup granulated sugar
1 cup ice
Enough cold white wine to fill
    the melon; a dry sauvignon
    blanc works well
4 straws

1. Carefully slice a small piece off the bottom of the melon at the stem end, just enough for the melon to be able to stand upright. Cut another piece off the top, opening the melon like a jack-o-lantern. Make the hole large enough to fit a spoon.

2. Scoop out the seeds and discard.

3. Scrape the flesh from the inside, but leave it inside the melon.

4. Add the sugar and mix well, allow the sugar to dissolve before adding first the ice and then the wine to fill.

5. Insert the straws. Enjoy straight from the melon, passing it from person to person.

CLERY | *Chilean White Sangria*

SERVES 4

Clery (or clérico, as some people call it) is a summery white wine sangria served in Chile. We are privileged to have long afternoons in the summer, due to Chile's southern latitude. When the shadows are long and slanted, that's when it's time to put together this easy, refreshing drink. This version has sauvignon blanc and strawberries, which are the first of the berries to arrive in summer, and are harbingers of warm weather, jam making, and lots of time outside with family and friends.

Serve clery with salty snacks in whatever tumblers you have on hand, but we like it in a shortball glass, like you'd serve whiskey in. Serve it neat, though, unless you like your wine watery. This is a perfect drink to watch the sunset with, or as you're waiting for the meat to come off the grill.

2 cups sliced strawberries
3 tablespoons granulated sugar
1 bottle cold white wine
   (chardonnay or sauvignon
   blanc)

1. Mix the strawberries with the sugar in a pitcher and set aside for 20 minutes to allow the strawberries to macerate.

2. Add the wine. Stir and refrigerate for at least 2 hours; it will hold for up to 6 hours.

3. Serve cold.

PEBRE | *Chilean Salsa Fresca*

SERVES 8

Bread is a cornerstone of the Chilean table. And in place of butter, there's usually a terra-cotta bowl full of what looks like salsa fresca. This fresh salsa is called pebre, *and whatever you do, don't dip your bread into it. Instead, split your bread open, and use a spoon to scoop* pebre *on.*

If you happen to arrive early to a meal, it would not be unusual to be handed a knife, a tomato, an onion, and a cutting board for you to help with the pebre *prep. Though* pebre *is an important part of the meal, this is considered an entry-level task, so don't worry about it too much.*

The simplicity and combination of fresh ingredients mean that no matter who makes it, it will turn out delectable, and before the meal is over, it is likely to make its way onto bread, empanadas, meat, and many other dishes. A certain subset of people can be seen scooping the liquid that remains behind in the pebre *bowl as though it were soup. But we won't mention names.*

1 white or yellow onion

2 cups boiling water

1 bunch cilantro or 1 cup cilantro leaves

8 large tomatoes

½ sweet banana pepper or yellow Thai pepper

1 tablespoon red wine vinegar

1 tablespoon vegetable oil

½ teaspoon red chili sauce (harissa, sriracha, Tabasco, etc.)

Salt, to taste

1. Finely chop the onion, and place it in a bowl. Pour boiling water over it. Let sit for 10 minutes, then drain and rinse with cold water.

2. Pull the cilantro leaves from the stems. Discard stems. Chop leaves finely.

3. Quarter tomatoes, discarding seeds. Dice tomatoes.

4. Deseed and remove the membrane from the pepper and dice finely.

5. Place all ingredients into a nonreactive bowl. Stir well, and adjust seasoning to taste.

6. Serve right away or let sit in the refrigerator for a couple of hours before serving.

7. As a shortcut, you can process each ingredient separately in a food processor. Be careful not to overprocess. The result should be chunky, not liquidy.

BETARRAGAS RELLENAS
Layered Stuffed Beets
SERVES 4

This is a tasty, eye-catching use for leftover chicken (or you can buy a rotisserie chicken). The salad-type filling is not your US–style chicken salad. Instead, the chicken is chopped finely, so there's no trailing or falling chicken pieces as you cut the beets and scoop it into your mouth. It's pretty when served on a white plate, with contrasting layers of beets and chicken salad.

We can't emphasize enough how much better this dish is with freshly harvested beets. Look for beets with the tops still on, and leaves in good condition. Like so many vegetables, beets are sweetest when freshly picked, as storage gives time for sugars to turn to starch, which can give beets an earthy flavor. Make this dish year-round with beets, or substitute garden-fresh tomatoes at the height of summer.

4 medium beets
1 pound cooked chicken
3 tablespoons mayonnaise
2 tablespoons chopped chives
Salt, to taste
Pepper, to taste

1. Preheat the oven to 450°F.

2. Trim the roots and stems from the beets.

3. Wrap the beets in foil and roast until they can be easily pierced with a table knife, around 30 to 40 minutes. Let them cool.

4. Chop the cooked chicken in small pieces, to just short of minced.

5. Mix the chicken with the mayonnaise and chives. Add salt and pepper to your liking. Taste and adjust the seasoning.

6. Peel and cut the beets into flat, ½-inch slices, so they can be layered. Place a beet slice on the plate, cover it with a tablespoon of the chicken salad, repeat with two additional layers of beets, and finish each stack with a beet slice as the top layer.

ENSALADA CHILENA | *Chilean Salad*

SERVES 4

One of the things that typifies the Chilean table is that there are always multiple salads on offer. It is not unusual to have two or three different salads at a single meal at home, and when Chileans go out for local food, they order a few salads to share at the table. One of these is nearly always ensalada chilena.

It might surprise you to know that the national salad of Chile doesn't contain even a whisper of lettuce, and that Chileans wouldn't have it any other way. Its two main ingredients are tomatoes and onions, each with a prescribed cut, with the onions rinsed, so they are more crunch than bite. Strict traditionalists will peel their tomatoes, but we won't insist on that step. The juiciest tomatoes make the best ensalada chilena, *and it's not unusual at the end of a meal for someone to say* permiso *(excuse me), as they spoon out the liquid left behind to sprinkle on bread, or pour over the rest of the rice on their plate. Not a drop is wasted.*

1 yellow onion
4 cups boiling water
1 clove garlic (optional)
1 sweet banana pepper
  (optional)
5 medium-sized tomatoes
Salt
Pepper
Oil
Red or white wine vinegar

1. Cut onion in half lengthwise and slice thinly. Place in a bowl, cover with boiling water, and let stand for 10 minutes. Drain and rinse with cold water. Dry with paper towels.

2. Chop the garlic and seed the peppers and chop them finely.

3. Cut the tomatoes into wedges, place in a bowl, sprinkle with salt, and stir.

4. Add onion, garlic, and finely chopped pepper if desired.

5. Season with salt, pepper, oil, and vinegar.

6. Stir and taste. Adjust the seasoning.

POROTOS GRANADOS
Bean, Corn, and Squash Potage
SERVES 4

Mas chileno que los porotos *(more Chilean than beans)* is Chile's version of "as American as apple pie." *Simply put,* porotos *(beans) are the backbone of many hearty Chilean dishes, a tradition we owe to the original inhabitants of this land, like the Quechua speakers from whom we borrowed this word for beans.*

In what is now the United States, indigenous peoples have traditionally used the system of "three sisters" planting, sowing corn, beans, and squash together. Though this style of planting is not commonly known in Chile, it is these three key ingredients that are the base of one of Chile's most popular summer dishes, porotos granados.

In Chile, children learn to desgranar, *or pop the beans out of the pods. Older relatives de-kernel the corn for this dish in a messy process best done outside. The* coscorrón *beans we use in Chile are not available in the United States, so we suggest a substitute, and frozen or canned corn works perfectly. These few recipe adaptations to use ingredients available in the United States make this dish quicker and easier, without sacrificing any of the original flavor.*

2 tablespoons vegetable oil

1 teaspoon sweet paprika

1 yellow onion, cut in small cubes

2 cups winter squash, cubed, fresh or frozen, divided

2 cups frozen whole kernel golden corn

2 tomatoes, cubed

10 large leaves sweet basil, plus additional to garnish if desired

2 cups low-sodium vegetable broth

2 (15.5-oz) cans high-quality (not store-brand) white beans, drained and rinsed

Salt, to taste

Pepper, to taste

1. In a medium pot, over medium-high heat, heat 2 tablespoons of vegetable oil, add the paprika, and cook for 1 minute.

2. Add the onion and cook, stirring occasionally for 6 minutes.

3. Add one cup of the squash, along with the corn, tomatoes, basil, and broth. Reduce the heat to medium and cook for 10 minutes, uncovered.

4. Add the beans and the remaining squash, adjust the seasoning with salt and pepper, and garnish with fresh basil if desired. Serve hot.

PAILA MARINA | *Brothy Seafood Soup*

SERVES 4

Paila marina is another Chilean classic, though due to the number of ingredients, it is a bit more involved. You might think of it as a Chilean bouillabaisse, or fish stew. The bounty of the ocean is embodied here, Chile's rich coast being prime grounds for catching and harvesting fish, squid, mussels, and clams. The delicate broth is flavored with bay leaf, peppers, onions, oregano, and a nice white wine.

You'll most often find Chileans eating this over the weekend or during summer beach holidays, as a late lunch. No one is sure if the soporific effect is just from eating a big bowl of soup, or that it's packed full of mariscos (seafood). One thing for sure is that paila marina *practically requires a nap after eating it, which is why weekends are the perfect time for this distinctly Chilean soup. The* paila *refers to the terra-cotta bowl in which this dish is traditionally served, but any bowl will do. Use the freshest products you can find, and feel free to add shrimp or other seafood.*

1 pound fresh mussels in the
    shell, or ½ pound canned
    mussels
1 yellow onion
½ red bell pepper
1 pound whitefish or salmon
1 tablespoon vegetable oil
Salt, to taste
Pepper, to taste
1 teaspoon Mexican oregano
½ teaspoon sweet paprika
1 bay leaf
2 cups white wine
4 cups fish or vegetable broth
½ pound shrimp
½ pound calamari
Chopped parsley and lemon to
    serve

1. Clean the mussels thoroughly if fresh.
2. Cut the onion in half lengthwise and then slice thinly. Slice the pepper lengthwise into strips.
3. Cut the fish into 1½-inch cubes.
4. In a large pot, heat 1 tablespoon of oil over medium-high flame. Add the onion, bell pepper, salt, pepper, and the herbs. Cook for 5 minutes, stirring occasionally.
5. Add the wine and broth. Cook to boiling, lower the heat, and let simmer. After 10 minutes add the fish and mussels. Let cook for 5 more minutes. Discard any unopened mussels.
6. Add the shrimp and calamari. Cook until the shrimp is pink, about 3 minutes.
7. Serve hot, with a sprinkle of parsley and some lemon wedges.

QUINOTTO DE CALLAMPAS
Dried Porcini Quinoa
SERVES 4

While risotto is popular at Italian restaurants in Chile, it is not something many home cooks choose to make, as it is quite labor-intensive. This Chilean version uses quinoa and therefore requires much less stirring. Although quinoa is the ancestral grain of the Andes, it did not appear in major supermarkets in Chile until fairly recently. However, given rising interest in whole grains, quinoa has become a popular addition to many people's shopping lists, often prepared as a pilaf or as quinotto *(quinoa risotto).*

In this recipe the quinoa pairs beautifully with dried mushrooms, which have long been a staple in the Chilean kitchen. Dried mushrooms are so commonplace in Chile that they hang in little bags in the spice section at the supermarket. In Chile, there's an expression "vale callampa" (it's worth mushrooms) to mean something that has no real value. Which is ironic, because they are a highly valued ingredient that impart an earthy umami flavor.

1 package (15 grams) dried porcini mushrooms
1 cup boiling water
2 cups uncooked white quinoa
1 tablespoon vegetable oil
2 tablespoons unsalted butter, divided
1 medium yellow onion, diced
1 cup heavy whipping cream
½ cup shredded Parmesan cheese
2 tablespoons unsalted butter
Salt, to taste
Pepper, to taste

1. Soak the dried mushrooms in 1 cup of boiling water for 30 minutes, and then strain and dice them, reserving the mushroom water.

2. Cook the quinoa according to package instructions, and spread on a tray to cool.

3. Place a large skillet or pot over high heat, and add 1 tablespoon each of vegetable oil and butter.

4. Cook the onion until golden, about 8 minutes, stirring.

5. Add the cream, mushrooms and their reserved water, and the Parmesan cheese. Mix well.

6. Add the quinoa and remaining butter. Taste and adjust the seasoning with salt and pepper. Serve hot.

TALLARINES CON PALTA

Noodles with Avocado Pesto

SERVES 4

In Chile we use the word palta, *from the indigenous Quechua for avocado, literally, a hanging weight, as opposed to the Nahuatl-derived* aguacate *you may know from Spanish class. This dish might be proof that much like Californians, Chileans think that many foods are improved with the addition of avocado, which grows well in our soil.*

As late as the 1980s in Chile, avocado was available mostly only in-season, with varieties such as Edranol, Fuerte, and La Cruz, which has a nearly paper-thin, black skin. But the return of democracy in 1990 changed the economy and positioned Chile as an agricultural powerhouse, including production and export of the Hass avocado, which now dominates the world market. Some 30 percent of those avocados stay in Chile, and they grace many dishes. Here, they appear as a main ingredient for a pasta sauce you might think of as a version of salsa nogada *(a creamy walnut sauce from Spain), or even pesto. Make this dish immediately before serving.*

1 package (16 oz.) spaghetti
2 large ripe avocados
1 tablespoon lemon juice
½ cup cilantro leaves or sweet
   basil
1 garlic clove, minced
¼ cup walnuts
Salt, to taste
Pepper, to taste

1. Cook the spaghetti following the package directions.

2. Cut the avocados in half and scoop the flesh into a blender or food processor.

3. Add the lemon juice, cilantro or basil, garlic, walnuts, salt, and pepper. Blend until smooth.

4. Mix with the spaghetti and serve immediately. You'll want to clean your plate; this dish does not keep.

TOMATICÁN
Juicy Summery Tomato and Meat Sauté
SERVES 4

For many Chileans, tomaticán *is summer on a plate. It's a quick dish with bright flavors, perfect for eating after a hard morning's work. Though many might consider it a stew, the beef, the corn, and the tomatoes each maintain their integrity, and we like to think of it as more of a juicy sauté.*

Some people prefer tomaticán *with rice, and some prefer it with boiled potatoes, serving about ⅔ tomaticán to ⅓ starch. That much we can agree on. But the debate is on about whether* tomaticán *is best served over the starch (which the mixers insist on) or beside it (which separatists prefer). There are usually representatives of both camps in each family, and no one, in the history of Chile, has ever been able to convince anyone else that their way is the right way. As it is a quick and simple meal, in Chile it would be unusual to serve* tomaticán *to guests. But if you do, your guest might help to tip the delicate mixer/separatist ratio.*

1 pound top sirloin, cut in
    2-inch-long strips
Salt, to taste
Pepper, to taste
1 tablespoon vegetable oil
1 yellow onion, cut in half and
    then in thin slices
1 cup frozen whole kernel golden
    corn
3 tomatoes, cut in wedges
½ teaspoon ground cumin

1. Season the meat with salt and pepper.

2. In a medium skillet, heat 1 tablespoon of oil over medium-high flame. Add the meat and let it cook undisturbed for 2 minutes, then turn the pieces over and let them cook for 2 additional minutes. Remove meat from the skillet.

3. In the same skillet, heat 1 tablespoon oil and add the onion. Sauté for 6 minutes, stirring occasionally.

4. Add the corn, tomatoes (including juice), cumin, salt, and pepper. Cook for 5 minutes.

5. Add the meat with its juices and cook for 2 minutes. Adjust the seasoning and serve.

PASTEL DE CHOCLO
Ground Beef Casserole with Mashed Corn Topping
SERVES 8

There is not yet a consensus on the national dish of Chile, but this one would certainly be in the running. Pastel de choclo is Chile's version of shepherd's pie, the mashed potatoes swapped out for a hearty topping made of oversized, hearty Chilean corn.

We usually make pastel de choclo in the summer, when the first of this giant corn appears at the market, and when we can buy basil so fresh the roots are still attached. Because outside of this region, corn tends to be less starchy, this US-friendly recipe thickens the topping with cornstarch. But please don't even dream of trading out the fresh basil for dried.

In Chilean restaurants, where pastel de choclo is frequently on the menu, it will arrive bubbling hot to the table in individual terra-cotta bowls. Most people start at the edge, using a spoon to break through the crunchy top layer to reveal the steamy interior filled with seasoned ground beef and studded with pieces of egg, raisins, and olives.

For the filling
2 tablespoons vegetable oil
2 pounds ground beef
Salt, to taste
Pepper, to taste
1 tablespoon paprika or *merkén*
½ teaspoon ground cumin
1 cup water or beef broth
3 medium yellow onions, finely
   chopped
2 tablespoons all-purpose flour

For the corn mash
2 tablespoons butter
10 cups frozen corn
½ cup whole milk
1 small bunch sweet basil
Salt, to taste
Pepper, to taste
Paprika or *merkén*
1 tablespoon cornstarch dissolved
   in ¼ cup cold milk or water

For assembly
8 pitted black olives
16 raisins
2 hard-boiled eggs

1. **Make the filling:** Heat the oil in a large skillet over medium-high heat. Add the whole package of meat at once (don't break it up), season with salt and pepper. Cook for 3 minutes. Flip it over, season with salt, pepper, paprika, and cumin and cook for an additional 3 minutes. The meat should be browned.

2. Add the broth and simmer 30 minutes over low heat, stirring occasionally

3. Add the onions and mix well. Cook over medium heat until the onions are tender, 30 minutes, stirring occasionally.

4. Turn off heat. Adjust seasoning if necessary. Add the flour and stir well.

5. **Make the corn mash:** Melt the butter in a large pot over medium-high heat. Add the frozen corn and stir. Cook 8 minutes.

6. Add the milk, basil, salt, pepper, and paprika or *merkén* or paprika, and continue to cook, stirring occasionally for 10 minutes.

7. Puree the corn using an immersion blender or working in batches in a blender or food processor.

8. Do not puree it smooth, but leave some larger pieces. Add the dissolved cornstarch and continue cooking over medium heat 5 minutes. Taste and adjust seasoning. It will thicken slightly.

9. **To assemble the pie:** Preheat the oven to 400°F. Spread the meat in a 9 x 13-inch baking dish. Dot the top of the meat with the olives, raisins, and halved (or sliced) hard-boiled eggs, spacing them evenly.

10. Cover with the corn mixture, smooth the top with a spatula, and then sprinkle with granulated sugar.

11. Bake for 45 to 60 minutes until bubbling and golden on top. Let cool 10 minutes before serving.

BERENJENAS RELLENAS | *Stuffed Eggplant*

SERVES 4

There are many Chilean dishes borrowed from other parts of the world. Here, we take the Middle Eastern tradition of stuffing vegetables like eggplant or zucchini and make it our own. Stuffed eggplant is a great everyday meal, and a good way to use up leftover rice. This dish is often made with zucchini instead of eggplant.

In a way, eggplant in Chile is thought of like liver is in the United States, which is to say it is reviled by some, though usually because they've had a bad experience with it. In Chile eggplant is a food that people use as a barometer of things they think taste unpleasant. "Es como las berenjenas" (it's like eggplant) is a way to say that it's something you don't like. In the case of eggplant, this is probably mainly due to the fact that when the plant is stressed, the fruit becomes bitter. With modern agriculture and the use of drip irrigation, you are much less likely to find a bitter eggplant than in years past. We might have to come up with a new Chilean expression!

2 medium eggplants (about 1 pound)
1 (15-oz.) can tomato sauce
1 cup water
Salt, to taste
Pepper, to taste
2 tablespoons vegetable oil
1 pound ground beef (90% lean, or 85% lean for a more decadent meal)
Cumin
1 carrot, diced finely
1 medium yellow onion, diced finely
1 garlic clove, minced
1 (14.5-oz.) can diced tomatoes
2 cups cooked long-grain rice
4 slices Muenster or Havarti cheese

1. Preheat the oven to 350°F.

2. Cut each eggplant lengthwise, and make them into 4 "boats." The best way to do this is to run your knife around the edge, leaving a ¼-inch border, and then cut and scoop the middle part away. Dice the scooped-out eggplant flesh.

3. Line a half sheet pan with parchment paper, and pour the tomato sauce and water in it. Lay the eggplant halves on top, face up. Season the eggplant boats with salt and pepper.

4. In a large skillet over medium heat, warm 2 tablespoons of vegetable oil. Add the meat and brown 3 minutes on each side. Break the meat down with a wooden spoon and season with salt, pepper, and ½ teaspoon of cumin.

5. Add the carrot, removed diced eggplant flesh, onion, garlic, and the can of diced tomatoes to the skillet. Cook for 5 minutes. Add the cooked rice and season to taste with salt and pepper.

6. Fill the eggplant halves with the ground beef and rice mixture.

7. Cover each stuffed eggplant with a slice of cheese and bake until bubbly and brown, about 30 minutes.

8. Serve hot.

LECHE ASADA DE DAMASCOS
Baked Milk and Apricot Pudding
SERVES 8

For the most part, the Chilean adult's diet doesn't include much dairy. But when it comes to desserts, the switch suddenly flips. Chilean desserts are gloriously creamy, and puddings and milky confections satisfy many a post-meal sweet tooth.

Leche asada is a creamy dessert not unlike flan, though it's a little less fussy, making it an easy midweek treat. While flan is made in a water bath, leche asada is baked directly in a dish in the oven. This makes for a less silky texture and a thin, firm layer around the edges, which is many people's favorite part.

While this dessert can be served without fruit, pairing it with apricots as we do here comes from a certain summer necessity. Just as zucchini goes crazy every summer in much of the United States, apricot trees in the central zone of Chile show homeowners no mercy. Each tree may yield dozens of kilos of apricots over the span of a few weeks. Here we suggest capturing a taste of summer by using some apricot jam, which also helps to cut the sweetness of the custard.

1 cup granulated sugar
½ cup water
5 eggs
3 cups whole milk
1 (13-oz.) jar apricot jam

1. Preheat the oven to 350°F.

2. In a small saucepan, over medium-high heat, cook the sugar and water together until the syrup begins to change color.

3. Lower the heat to low and as soon as the liquid turns light brown, carefully pour it into an 8x8-inch ovenproof baking dish. Using oven mitts, slowly tilt the dish, so the caramel covers the whole bottom and lower sides.

4. In a bowl, thoroughly whisk together eggs and milk.

5. Add the jam and mix.

6. Pour the mixture over the caramel and bake for 45 minutes or until the top is browned.

7. Let cool and refrigerate.

8. Serve cold.

DURAZNOS CON CREMA
Stewed Peaches (with Cream)
SERVES 8

If there were a competition, we'd like to nominate this dish for being about the most Chilean dessert we can think of. In Chile, we make it with canned peaches and canned cream. It's a traditional dessert served on high school class trips, and if you play bingo in a small town, you could well win a can of each if you have a lucky cartón *(bingo card).*

   While in general, people view it as declassé, it is so imbued into the childhood of nearly every Chilean that they'll probably scoop every sugary drop out of the bowl. It can also be a barometer of how confident a cook you are. For inexperienced dessert-makers, canned peaches with cream is 100 percent reliable, and one often has the ingredients already on hand. Here we've reimagined this dish with aromatic fresh stewed peaches, cooked with pisco, sugar, and cloves. The truly Chilean version is with canned cream, but we know you're going to serve it with vanilla ice cream. You have our blessings.

½ cup pisco or vodka
2 cups water
1½ cups granulated sugar
4 whole cloves
8 yellow peaches, still firm
Crema Nestlé (canned), or
   vanilla ice cream

1. In a medium skillet, mix the pisco, water, sugar, and cloves. Stir.

2. Cook over medium-high heat until it boils, about 5 minutes. Reduce the heat to a simmer.

3. Cut the peaches in half and remove the pits. Place the peaches flat in the simmering syrup. Cook 8 minutes, flip them over, and cook 3 additional minutes until cooked, but not soft.

4. Remove the peaches, let cool enough to handle, and remove the skins.

5. Let the syrup reduce to about half. Let cool and remove the cloves.

6. Serve peaches and syrup together with a dollop of Crema Nestlé or vanilla ice cream.

Fall

Fall in central Chile is marked mainly by the end of summer and then the slow slide into winter. We tend to have warm days throughout the fall, though a nighttime and early morning chill can creep in, making for days of carrying around scarves and jackets at midday. Responsibilities pick up, as we return to the regular rhythm of city life and pack kids off to school in this year's uniforms, with new notebooks and textbooks in tow.

Weekends in fall feel like a gift, with snippets of free time to spend out and about in the slanting autumn sunshine, turning our faces to catch a few more rays. And after the urban summer calm, public spaces fill up with families, kids asking for a few coins to rent pedal cars they can ride around plazas and parks. And no weekend is complete without a stop at the *cuchuflí* (coo-choo-FLEE) vendor, buying these rolled wafers filled fresh with dulce de leche (otherwise they can get soggy). They come four or five in a bag, and having a bag for yourself feels indulgent.

In fall, the vegetable selection at the *feria* changes, with giant sawed-open squash just waiting to be picked up and taken home for stews and soups, chestnuts to be made into a caramel-scented puree, to be served with fresh whipped cream. Fall is also when winemakers roll through their harvest, picking in turn the grapes for first white, then later red wines, to be crushed, fermented, and turned into one of Chile's most famous exports, though we consume a fair amount locally as well.

There is no main holiday that anchors fall, though many consider a last hurrah at the beach during *Semana Santa* (Holy Week) to be a farewell to warmer temperatures and longer days. From here on out, we'll hold onto our coffee and tea mugs just a little while longer, while we wait for winter, our coziest season, to begin.

Fall

NAVEGADO | *Mulled Red Wine*

SERVES 4

Navegado is Chile's version of mulled wine, a spiced, sweet, warm drink with all the flavors of cooler days. When handed a mug, nearly everyone cups it in their hands and inhales the cinnamon-clovey goodness before taking a sip. In Chile it's perfect after a day out in the countryside, whether working or playing. For someone who's come in from outside entumido *(numb from the cold) or* calado hasta los huesos *(chilled to the bone), it's the perfect antidote. And at a campfire or a nighttime barbecue, it's a warming concoction to share. In Chile it is served to children as young as 10 or 12, as much of the alcohol cooks off.*

This is probably the only alcoholic beverage for which we would not say salud *(cheers) before drinking. Perhaps that's because it's served informally, from a pot, and everyone starts drinking it at different times, or because clinking mugs is just not done. Also bucking the tradition, whereas Chileans generally won't use their hands to eat, you might catch the cook eating a slice of the wine-infused fruit before serving. You could make a summer version by icing* navegado. *It's no longer a well-guarded secret that it tastes great cold.*

2 navel oranges
6 cloves
1 (25.4-oz.) bottle cabernet
  sauvignon
½ cup granulated sugar
4 cinnamon sticks

1. Leave the rind on the oranges, and slice each into ½-inch-thick slices. Pop out and discard the seeds. Stud the orange rinds with the cloves.

2. In a pot over medium heat, mix all the ingredients and stir until the sugar dissolves.

3. Let it boil 2 minutes, reducing to a simmer if you need to keep it warm before serving.

4. Serve hot.

SALSA VERDE | *Parsley-Onion Salsa*

SERVES 4

Do not confuse this with Mexico's completely different tomatillo-based sauce of the same name. Chile's salsa verde *is similar to a chunky vinaigrette, and stands in for a chutney, providing a tangy counterpoint to milder flavors.* Salsa verde *normally appears in a small, deep bowl with a spoon in it, to be shared at the table, and scooped over food. Chileans historically have not been much for dipping into sauces, and even the most traditional* Pebre/Chilean Salsa Fresca *(page 23) is scooped onto food or bread, rather than dipped into.*

This parsley-based sauce is perfect for spooning on top of nearly whatever food you like. At a Sunday meal, you might find people using it atop papas mayo *(a type of potato salad). In Chile, it's probably also the main use of parsley, which is always sold by the bunch, and is often next to the cilantro. Handily, the same mnemonic that works to remember which is which in English (parsley is pointy, cilantro is curvy) works in Spanish, too* (perejil tiene puntas, cilantro tiene curvas). *For the onion, use your judgment. If it's extra pungent, you might want to give it a rinse after chopping and before using, otherwise, you can skip this step.*

½ medium yellow onion
2 bunches parsley
2 tablespoons freshly squeezed
   lemon juice
2 tablespoons vegetable oil
Salt, to taste

1. Mince the onion and place it in a bowl. Optionally, pour boiling water over it and let it stand for 3 minutes. Rinse it in a strainer under cold water.

2. Strip the parsley leaves from the stems and chop finely, discarding the stems.

3. Combine the onion, parsley, lemon juice, and oil. Add salt to taste.

4. Serve immediately or let it sit for up to a couple of hours in the refrigerator before serving.

ENSALADA DE REPOLLO CON ZANAHORIA
Cabbage and Carrot Salad
SERVES 4

Cabbage is inexpensive, easy to grow, and filling. It keeps well even without refrigeration, and you can rely on finding it all year round in both Chile and the United States.

Here, green cabbage is prepared as a colorful salad, speckled with shredded carrots. Though it takes a certain skill to slice the cabbage thinly enough for many Chileans' taste, your crowd may not be so hard to please. If you have a mandoline, it will save you loads of trouble. Think of this salad as a kind of non-mayonnaise-dressed slaw, and although we'd normally eat it as part of an array of salads for a main meal, it stands up really well as a simple side dish. It provides the perfect crunch to complement stews like Zapallo con Mote/Hearty Winter Squash with Barley *(page 61).*

½ medium green cabbage
3 large carrots
2 lemons
1 tablespoon vegetable oil
Salt, to taste

1. Use a mandoline on the finest setting to slice the cabbage. Discard the core. Place the shredded cabbage in a bowl of ice water and let it sit for 10 minutes.

2. Peel the carrots and use the coarse side of a box grater to grate them.

3. Strain the water off the cabbage, add the carrots to the bowl, and season with the lemon juice, oil, and salt.

4. Let sit at least 30 minutes before serving.

CREMA DE GARBANZOS | *Creamy Chickpea Soup*
SERVES 4

In Chile, beans, chickpeas, and lentils could use some good PR. Maybe it's because we associate them with leaner times, or country living. Either way, it's not uncommon to hear one child warn another before inviting them to come over for a meal, that it's legume day. In most traditional Chilean homes, legumes are served once or twice a week, whether lentils, beans, or chickpeas (though in Chile, these are never mixed together). This soup would often be made from leftover chickpea stew from the day before, and more than one child who "doesn't like garbanzos" has downed a bowl at lunch or dinner.

This creamy chickpea soup can easily be prepared vegetarian, but in many homes, a longaniza, *(sausage) is served on top. The sausage is cooked separately, fried in a skillet, and not stewed together with the chickpeas. Soups like this are the harbingers of shorter days and colder nights, when a bowl of hearty warm soup hits the spot.*

1 medium yellow onion
1 tablespoon vegetable oil
1 teaspoon sweet paprika or
   merkén
½ teaspoon ground cumin
Salt, to taste
2 (16-oz.) cans chickpeas
2 cups low-sodium vegetable
   broth
1 bay leaf
2 Spanish chorizos, optional

1. Chop the onion into rough dice.
2. In a medium pot, over medium-high heat, add 1 tablespoon of oil and the onion. Cook, stirring occasionally for 6 to 8 minutes. Add the paprika or *merkén*, salt, and cumin, and stir to mix and cook for 1 minute. Lower the heat to medium.
3. Drain the chickpeas (don't rinse) and add them to the pot with the vegetable broth and the bay leaf.
4. Cover and simmer for 15 minutes.
5. Remove the bay leaf and, using an immersion blender or working in batches in a jug blender, puree the soup.
6. Serve hot.

Note: if using the chorizo, cook in a skillet following the package instructions, and cut each in half, and place on top of the soup before serving.

TORTILLA DE LECHUGA
Stove-Top Lettuce Frittata
SERVES 4

Lettuce has experienced a revolution in recent years, with more compact lettuce falling to the bottom of the list and lighter, fluffier lettuces making up many people's salads. Here's a callback to large, hearty romaine lettuce, but with a twist. As you may have noticed, Chileans are not fans of eating cold food in cooler weather. But lettuce is still in season in the fall, so here's the perfect solution. We take a whole head of romaine lettuce, slice it thinly, and fold it into one of the comodines (reliable standbys) popular in many Chilean kitchens, the (egg-based) tortilla. In the tortilla the lettuce wilts, but maintains its mild flavor.

A tortilla is similar to a frittata, though it is cooked on the stove top, and this style of cooking is also on loan from Spain, where the tortilla de patatas is quite common. In Chile this preparation is an old trick for getting everyone to eat their veggies and is usually served as a side dish.

1 large head romaine lettuce
3 eggs
2 tablespoons whole milk
Salt, to taste
Pepper, to taste
1 tablespoon vegetable oil

1. Wash the romaine leaves and cut out the ribs. Slice the leaves into thin strips.

2. In a large bowl, whisk the eggs and the milk vigorously for 30 seconds until well mixed. Add salt and pepper to taste.

3. Mix the lettuce into the eggs.

4. Heat 1 tablespoon of vegetable oil in a medium 9-inch nonstick skillet. Pour in lettuce and egg mixture and pat the lettuce down so it lies flat. Cook over medium heat for 8 to 10 minutes until firm. Flip and cook 3 to 5 minutes to finish.

5. You can also finish the tortilla in the oven using the broil function and avoid having to flip the tortilla. Just be sure to use a skillet with an ovenproof handle.

ZAPALLO CON MOTE
Hearty Winter Squash with Barley
SERVES 4

In Chile, wheat makes an appearance at nearly every meal, most often in the form of bread. We are so attached to wheat that we even have a late summer festival for its harvest, called the trilla a yegua suelta, *in which unbridled horses run circles around a corral set up for them to thresh the wheat by trampling it.*

But we don't only eat wheat flour in Chile. We also eat mote, *which is hulled wheat berries, and its most frequent appearance is in a beverage/dessert called* Mote con Huesillos/Sweetened Dried Peach Punch with Barley *(page 131). In this squash-and-wheat-berry preparation, the* mote *gives a little bite to what would otherwise be an entirely soft dish. It makes the perfect contrast to the buttery texture of the squash we use in Chile, a Peter-Peter-Pumpkin-Eater-sized squash whose closest correlate in the United States is the Cinderella squash. Use butternut squash and canned pumpkin if that's easier to find. And while you can use the traditional wheat berries if you can find them, barley makes a fine substitute if it's easier for you to get.*

6 cups water
Salt, to taste
1 cup barley
1 medium yellow onion, diced
1 tablespoon vegetable oil
1 (15-oz.) can pumpkin
1 tablespoon sweet paprika
Pepper, to taste
1 (16-oz.) bag frozen butternut
    squash

1. In a medium pot, bring 6 cups of water to boiling and add a generous pinch of salt. Add the barley and cover, lowering the heat. Cook 15 minutes. Drain and rinse under cold water.

2. The barley will still have some bite to it. You can cook and refrigerate the barley up to a few days in advance.

3. In a large skillet over medium-high heat, sauté the onion in 1 tablespoon of vegetable oil for 6 to 8 minutes. Lower the heat to medium, and add the pumpkin, paprika, salt, and pepper. Mix well. Add the frozen butternut squash and cooked barley.

4. Cover and let it all cook together 5 minutes, stirring occasionally. Check that the frozen squash is warmed through before taking off the heat. Adjust the seasoning.

5. Serve hot.

TARTA PASCUALINA DE ESPINACAS
Double-Crusted Spinach Pie
SERVES 8

According to many chefs, Chileans borrowed this dish from our neighbors across the Andes, in Argentina. It probably was an easy import, given the facility with which Chileans in the south took to sweet pies, which we call kuchen. *Filling a similar pastry with savory creamy spinach was not a big leap. Though of course, we put our own spin on it, taking the liberty of switching out ricotta and eggs—which to us seem more like the inside of a ravioli, and which yield a lumpier filling—and replacing them with a creamy béchamel sauce for a smoother texture. This aligns better with the Chilean preference for smooth foods over those with lumps.*

Pascualina makes a very pretty first course or side dish, and because it is so attractive and travels and keeps well, it is a welcome dish at any potluck. While we love the spinach version, the tarta pascualina de alcachofas *(with an artichoke filling) also holds a special place in our hearts.* Pascualina *can be served at room temperature or warm.*

4 (10-oz.) boxes frozen spinach, defrosted
1 medium yellow onion
1 tablespoon vegetable oil
4 tablespoons unsalted butter
¾ cup all-purpose flour
2 cups whole milk
1 box refrigerated or frozen piecrust
Salt, to taste
Pepper, to taste
Nutmeg, optional
4 hard-boiled eggs, peeled and cut in half

1. Using a strainer, squeeze the water out of the spinach, and chop coarsely.

2. Chop the onion to small dice.

3. In a large skillet over medium heat, warm the oil, add the onion, and cook, stirring occasionally, for 10 minutes. Add the chopped spinach and cover. Cook 3 minutes. Place the cooked spinach mixture in a bowl.

4. Wipe the skillet and add butter. Melt butter over medium heat. Add the flour, stir with a fork, and cook for 2 minutes. Remove from the heat, and add the milk slowly and mix it well, so no lumps remain. Once all the milk is added, return to the heat, and continue stirring until it comes to a boil. Lower the heat so it simmers for 1 minute. Season with salt, pepper, and optional nutmeg.

5. Add the cooked spinach and onion to the sauce and mix well. The filling should be thick. Taste and adjust seasonings.

6. Preheat the oven to 350°F.

7. Butter a 9-inch springform pan. Unroll one of the piecrusts and cover the bottom, pressing the dough up the sides. Unroll the second crust, cut off about ¾-inch around the edge, and use that dough to finish lining the walls of the pan. Layer ⅔ of the spinach filling on top. Arrange the hard-boiled eggs symmetrically, in a radiating pattern, and top with the rest of the spinach filling. Use the remaining circle of dough to cover the pie, crimping the edge with your fingers.

8. Cut a small vent in the center of the top pie crust to allow the steam to escape.

9. Place the pie dish on top of a baking sheet and bake for 45 to 60 minutes until the dough is golden and the filling is bubbling.

10. Take the *pascualina* out of the oven and place on a cooling rack. Allow it to cool for half an hour before slicing and serving.

PICANTE DE CAMARONES | *Tomato Shrimp Stew*
SERVES 4

Stewy picante de camarones *combines one of Chile's favorite flavors — the tomato — with succulent shrimp. The resulting dish has the texture of a curry, and for many Chileans, in addition to* ají de gallina, *is a go-to dish on Peruvian menus. But if it comes to us from Peru, then why include it in this book about Chilean food?*

Peru borders with Chile to the north, and Peruvians have come to live in Chile throughout our countries' histories. Given our coexistence, we have had a long time to fall in love with Peruvian food, and lucky for us this dish doesn't require any ingredients that are difficult to find in Chile or the United States.

The other reason we include this dish here is because many people feel that the wild popularity of Peruvian food in Chile played a role in shaping Chileans' appreciation for our own food. In a way, it encouraged a deeper dive into our own culinary identity and breathed life into the current movement of revindicando los sabores chilenos *(reclaiming Chilean flavors) as a point of national pride.*

1 medium yellow onion, chopped
1 tablespoon vegetable oil
1 garlic clove, minced
⅓ cup chopped walnuts
1 teaspoon sweet paprika
1 sweet banana pepper or Thai
  pepper, seeded and chopped
1 (14.5-oz.) can diced tomatoes
¼ cup white wine (optional)
1 cup vegetable broth (or
  1¼ cups vegetable broth if
  omitting wine)
¼ cup cornstarch
¼ cup heavy whipping cream
3 slices Havarti cheese
36 large shrimp, deveined, with
  tails
Salt, to taste
Pepper, to taste

1. In a large (nonreactive) skillet over medium-high heat, cook the onion in 1 tablespoon of oil for 5 minutes. Add the garlic and walnuts and cook, stirring continuously, for 2 minutes. Lower the heat to medium.

2. Add the paprika, pepper, and tomatoes. Stir and cook for 3 minutes. Remove from the stove.

3. Pour the wine and broth into a 2-cup measuring cup. Dissolve the cornstarch in this mixture, and then pour it into a blender, along with the cream.

4. Add skillet contents into the blender and blend until pureed.

5. Return the blended mixture to the skillet over medium heat, cooking until it begins to bubble. Cook for 1 additional minute, and add the cheese. When it has melted, stir to mix and then add the shrimp. Cook until the shrimp is done, 3 to 5 minutes. Taste and adjust the seasoning. The resulting sauce should be thick.

6. Serve hot with white rice.

POLLO ESCABECHADO | *Pickled Chicken Thighs*

SERVES 4

Chile owes its gastronomy to a variety of sources, and the food is commonly referred to as mestiza, *to reflect that history. This dish clearly traces back to Spanish origin, where fowl was served* escabechado *(in a sauce flavored with wine and vinegar). In Spain this dish is served cold, but somewhere in translation, Chileans started serving it warm.*

In Chile, this country dish would traditionally be made with quail. Until about the 1990s, there was quite a bit of wild scrubland in central Chile. The thickets and brambles of the central valley and the occasional agricultural fields which had gone fallow were a perfect habitat for many animals, including quail. Nowadays, much of this land has been given over to agriculture, and fields are in near-constant use. At the same time, hunting has fallen in popularity.

Here we make the dish with chicken because these days quail is harder to come by both in Chile and in the United States. There is no mistaking the rich broth and falling-off-the-bone chicken for any other dish, neither in its beautiful aroma nor its distinctive taste.

8 chicken thighs, with bones
   and skin
Salt, to taste
Pepper, to taste
1 tablespoon white wine vinegar
1 cup sauvignon blanc
1 teaspoon sweet paprika
1 teaspoon dried Mexican
   oregano
2 bay leaves
Seville orange leaves, optional
2 medium yellow onions
3 carrots
1 tablespoon vegetable oil
1 cup water

1. Season the chicken with salt and pepper.
2. Use a bag or baking dish to marinate the chicken with the vinegar, wine, paprika, oregano, bay leaves, and orange leaves. Let sit overnight in the fridge.
3. Cut the onions in half lengthwise and then slice thinly. Peel the carrots and slice into ⅛-inch rounds.
4. Heat the oil in a big deep pot. Brown the chicken 3 minutes on each side. Add the onions, carrots, and the marinade. Mix and add the water. Cook for 20 minutes over medium-low heat until the chicken is tender.
5. Remove the leaves before serving. Serve with the vegetables and sauce spooned over the chicken.

SÉMOLA CON LECHE | *Semolina Pudding*

SERVES 8

Sémola con leche *is a rich, creamy dessert topped with a caramel sauce that brings back early memories for many Chileans. The* sémola *is semolina, which you may have eaten as cream of wheat or farina when you were a child in the United States. In Chile it's cooked into a thick milky pudding served cold and molded like* panna cotta *in the summer, and sumptuous and warm in the winter, eaten out of a bowl. It's many people's first dessert memory, one that brings them back to long family meals served at the homes of grandmothers who cooked with aprons on.*

Sémola con leche is popular with people of all ages, from the very young to full-fledged adults. Even where there's a corporate cafeteria, it wouldn't be unusual to see grown men and women choosing this among all other offered desserts, and savoring every bite before returning back to work. Make extra caramel and pour over right before serving for a crunchy-smooth sensory combo and a bit of extra sweetness.

For the caramel
1 cup granulated sugar
¼ cup water

For the pudding
4 cups whole milk
1 teaspoon vanilla extract
½ cup granulated sugar
¾ cup semolina

1. **For the caramel:** Place the sugar and water in a small pot. Warm over medium heat, stirring occasionally, making sure to dissolve all the sugar. Stop stirring and bring the syrup to a boil. When the mixture begins to change color, lower the heat and keep an eye on it, heating until it is the color of weak black tea or caramel candy. Divide the caramel between 8 ramekins. Cover the bottom and tilt each ramekin so the caramel coats halfway up the side.

2. **For the pudding:** In a medium pot, mix the milk, vanilla, and sugar. Cook over medium-high heat, stirring until the sugar dissolves and the liquid starts boiling. Lower the heat and add the semolina in a slow stream while you whisk vigorously. It will thicken quickly, but don't stop whisking. Allow it to come to a boil and cook for 1 minute, stirring continuously.

3. Pour the mixture into the prepared ramekins and smooth the top with the back of a spoon.

4. Let cool and refrigerate for a couple of hours.

5. To unmold, fill a large pan halfway with boiling water and place the ramekins in water. Allow the caramel to melt about 10 minutes. Invert each ramekin onto a dessert plate.

SUSPIRO DE MONJA | *Fried Choux Pastry*
SERVES 6

Though you may think you already know fried dough in all its forms, such as funnel cake, elephant ears, beignets, and churros, as versions of carnival food, Chile's version of this colonial dessert—called suspiro de monja*—is served mainly at home. It's a stiff dough, much like that for a profiterole (cream puff), and the resulting dough balls are airy, light, and melt in your mouth.*

These are usually served in groups of two or three, with some kind of syrup. We like them with Miel de Melón/Honeydew Syrup *(page 171),* miel de palma, *or powdered sugar sifted on top. The result is a sweet confection that you will want to eat as soon as it is cool enough to handle.* Suspiro de monja *is a weekend treat, usually served mid-afternoon.*

The name suspiro de monja *(literally, "nun's sigh") brings to mind two things. One, to have a "mano de monja" (literally, "nun's hand") means you're good with sweet treats. But why* suspiro? *We suspect this recognizes the ephemeral quality of this hot-fried treat, which, much like a sigh, is soon gone.*

½ cup water
4 tablespoons unsalted butter
½ teaspoon salt
2 teaspoons granulated sugar
½ cup all-purpose flour
2 large eggs
2 cups vegetable oil for frying

1. In a medium pot mix the water, butter, salt, and sugar. Bring to boil over medium-high heat, stirring occasionally, ensuring that the butter melts completely.

2. Remove from the heat and add the flour, then mix vigorously with a whisk or fork. Return to the heat and cook, stirring continuously, until the dough pulls away from the side of the pot.

3. Remove from the heat and let cool for 6 minutes.

4. Add the eggs one at a time, stirring briskly until a glossy dough forms.

5. Heat the oil in a large pot until it reaches 350°F. Drop 1 tablespoon of dough at a time, being careful not to overcrowd the pot. Fry them for 2 to 3 minutes and then flip them and fry 2 additional minutes.

6. Scoop them out with a slotted spoon and place on a plate lined with paper towels to drain.

7. Serve warm with sweet syrup or dusted with powdered sugar.

Winter

When winter arrives in earnest, with its shorter days and cooler temperatures, everything takes on a different time line. It gets dark early, and most people's first thought when they get out of work is that they can't wait to get home for the night. Where possible, we shift errands to lunchtime, shopping for birthday gifts and other essentials during daylight hours.

While the temperatures are not that low in central Chile (below-freezing temperatures are newsworthy), homes do not generally have central heating, and are better conditioned to the warmer months. In short, we are aware of the outside temperatures, because it is not that much warmer inside. Given this, we tend to gravitate toward the kitchen. And we load up our plates with the flavors of the season, broccoli and cabbage and cauliflower taking over for the more delicate greens we associate with warmer weather.

Due to the cool temperatures, turning on the oven is a treat, and some of the most delicious baked goods come out of this winter luxury of heating the home and stomach at the same time. The kettle is nearly always on, whether to make tea, or to add a little humidity to the air, especially where woodstoves are used for heat.

Winter is also the perfect time for industrious pursuits, and people break out their knitting, and even some old-school artisan work, which in some regions consists of making tiny figurines out of *crin* (horsehair) or weaving straw into *chupallas* (flat-brimmed straw hats). We do this beside the stove or heater, always with a mug of tea or coffee within reach.

August seems to be the coldest month, and one of the rainiest, too. Rains are sparse in some parts of Chile, but nearly always come in winter. When it rains, you can depend on a few things: slower transport, traffic jams, and people flooding social media with images of rainy day–worthy snacks and meals like *sopaipillas pasadas* (fried dough drenched in brown sugar syrup).

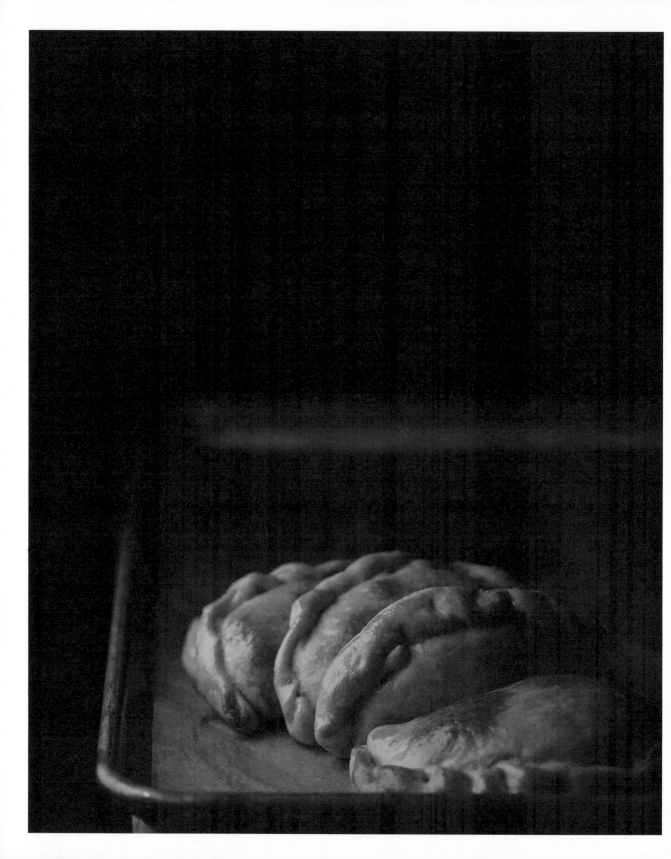

Winter

SOPAIPILLAS | *Squash-Flavored Fried Dough*

MAKES 20 *SOPAIPILLAS*

On rainy days in Santiago, social media is flooded with talk of sopaipillas pasadas, *homemade squash-flavored fried dough in a brown sugar syrup. Many Chileans have childhood memories of rainy days in the kitchen, making the dough, rolling it out, piercing it with a fork, and frying it. In the central region of Chile, where squash is always included (which is not the case in other parts of Chile), rains are infrequent and well-announced, giving home cooks lots of time to prepare the squash before kids come home from school.*

The afternoon snack of fried dough in a sweet sauce is just one way of eating sopaipillas*. We also like them plain or with powdered sugar, and nowadays many people like them savory, with Pebre/Chilean Salsa Fresca (page 23), including before a meal at restaurants. Avocado is another popular topping, and we've even heard of people topping them with canned mackerel and onions. Like a few other foods in Chile, this one shares its name with another dish — Tex-Mex* sopaipilla *— but the similarity stops there. And most Chileans wouldn't guess it, but we inherited the word* sopaipilla *indirectly from the Arabic, and* sopaipillas *came to Chile via Spanish colonization.*

2 cups all-purpose flour
2 teaspoons baking powder
1 teaspoon salt
1 cup pumpkin puree
3 tablespoons lard, shortening,
  or butter, melted
Vegetable oil for frying

1. In a food processor, pulse together the flour, baking powder, and salt.

2. Add the pumpkin and lard. Pulse it until a soft dough forms.

3. Place the dough on a plate, cover it with a tea towel, and let it rest for 20 minutes.

4. Working on a floured surface, roll the dough to ¼-inch thickness.

5. Cut into 3-inch circles, using a glass or biscuit cutter.

6. Prick with a fork 3 times each.

7. Heat at least 2 inches of oil in a deep pot, until it reaches 350°F.

8. Working in small batches, 4 to 5 at a time, fry the *sopaipillas* 2 to 3 minutes each side.

9. Remove to a plate lined with paper towels.

10. Serve hot with the topping of your choice.

PEQUENES | *Caramelized Onion Empanadas*
SERVES 6 (2 *PEQUENES* PER PERSON)

Empanadas arrived in the Americas with the Spaniards (likely from North Africa), and every country in Latin America has their own take on them. This is an old-school Chilean empanada that is an alternative to our meat-filled one, and though they're growing in popularity, pequenes *are found more in traditional* amasanderías *(bread shops) than at your casual corner store that also happens to sell empanadas.*

Pequenes (singular, pequén*) are filled with slow-cooked onions and pack a tender, sweet, cumin-infused bite. The dough is a bit different from that of meat empanadas, as the addition of an acidic element makes it more tender, a perfect contrast to the soft filling. Onions grow well in Chile, and show up in much of our food, so it's no surprise we have a savory pastry filled with almost nothing but.*

It is likely that the name pequén *came into use because in comparison to the Chilean meat empanada, they are quite small (*pequeño*), though some think this smaller empanada might have taken its name from the indigenous Mapuche word for an owl-like bird of prey, also called a* pequén*. Once considered the food of the poor,* pequenes *make a nice, lighter alternative to the meat empanada, and are easily made vegetarian.*

For the filling
2 tablespoons vegetable oil
3 large or 5 medium yellow onions, cut in half lengthwise and sliced thinly
1 teaspoon sugar
1 teaspoon salt
1 teaspoon paprika or *merkén*
Pepper, to taste
1 teaspoon ground cumin
1 teaspoon dried Mexican oregano
½ teaspoon hot sauce

For the dough
1¼ cups all-purpose flour
1½ teaspoons salt
1 teaspoon granulated sugar
2 tablespoons lard, shortening, or butter, cut in small cubes
¼ cup water
¼ cup whole milk
1 teaspoon lemon juice or apple cider vinegar
1 beaten egg, to seal and brush
Vegetable oil and pepper

1. **Make the filling:** Heat 2 tablespoons of oil in a large saucepan over medium heat. Add the onions, sugar, and salt.

2. Cook, stirring occasionally, for 30 minutes or until the onion is cooked, but only lightly caramelized.

3. Remove from heat and add paprika, pepper, cumin, oregano, and hot sauce. Taste and adjust the seasoning.

4. **Make the dough:** In a food processor, mix the flour, salt, and sugar. Pulse a couple of times. Add the lard or butter and pulse a few times until it is uniform.

5. In a measuring cup, mix the water, milk, and lemon juice. With the food processor running, add the liquid. Stop when you see the dough come together.

6. Knead the dough 10 minutes on a silicone baking mat or on a floured surface. Cover and let it rest 30 minutes.

7. Preheat the oven 350°F. Cover a baking sheet with parchment paper.

8. Divide the dough into 12 equal portions. Working one at a time, roll the dough into a ball, flatten it, and roll it with a rolling pin until you have a 5-inch circle.

9. Fill with 2 tablespoons of cooked onions. Wet the rim with the egg and seal shut, press the edge gently with a fork, or fold it over. Place on the baking sheet leaving an inch between *pequenes*.

10. Brush each empanada with egg and pierce the top with a toothpick to allow them to vent steam.

11. Bake for 25 to 30 minutes or until brown.

12. Let cool on a rack 10 minutes before serving.

ENSALADA DE POROTOS CON CEBOLLA

Bean and Onion Salad

SERVES 4

This cold bean salad is the winter sister to the summertime ensalada chilena, *which is made with most of the same ingredients, changing out beans for tomatoes. Beans are an integral part of the Chilean diet, but we mainly focus on only two kinds, a single variety of summer bean which is never dried, the* coscorrón *(see recipe for* Porotos Granados/Summer Bean Potage on page 29*), and one variety of winter/dried beans called* tórtola, *which are harvested dry from the stalk. Beans are nitrogen-fixing and good for the soil, so for many centuries Chileans have been enriching their soil by continuing the tradition of planting beans.*

This dish is prepared using the same cut of onions (long strips) as in the tomato salad, and we hate to buck tradition, but we think it would actually make more sense to dice them, to make it easier to eat. In that way it reminds us a bit of "Texas caviar," another cold bean salad you may already know and love. Make this one ahead of time to let the flavors marry, and to have one less thing to prepare just before the meal.

1 cup dried pinto beans
3 cups boiling water
1 teaspoon salt + more to taste
1 bay leaf
4 cups water
1 medium yellow onion
1 tablespoon vegetable oil
1 tablespoon lemon juice
Pepper
⅓ cup chopped parsley

1. Soak the beans overnight in a bowl with plenty of water.

2. Drain and remove any dirt or stones.

3. In a medium pot, cover the beans with the water, add the salt and bay leaf. Cook over medium heat. Once it boils, reduce it to a simmer and cook for 30 minutes.

4. Beans are ready when they are firm, but cooked (about 20 to 40 minutes).

5. Drain and let cool.

6. Cut the onion in half lengthwise and then slice thinly. Put in a bowl and blanch in boiling water for 10 minutes before rinsing under cold water and draining.

7. In a serving bowl, mix the beans and the onions, season with oil, lemon, salt, and pepper.

8. Sprinkle with the parsley and serve.

PANTRUCAS | *Country-Style Soup*
SERVES 4

The fact that no one is sure whether to call these simple, flat dumplings pantrucas *or* pancutras *makes their name a slippery operation. This jibes perfectly with the fact that they are hard to pin down in the bowl, often sliding off your spoon just before you get them to your mouth.*

This is a country dish, and the dumplings are often served in a thicker soup, made with collagen-rich bone broth, or in modern times, with ground meat as the base of the broth. In this way you can avoid having to chill the soup to pour off the fat. You can also thicken the broth with milk or eggs. In looking for a well-known correlate, what most easily comes to mind for the pantruca *is a meatless wonton or kreplach. The dough is dropped raw into a broth, and cooked until soft (beyond al dente).*

This soup would always be a starter, never a main course, and starter soups in Chile are always rich in broth and sparse on vegetables. Since pantrucas *tend to slide off the spoon, we prefer to cut them smaller than is traditional, but if you like a challenge, make yours larger.*

For the dough
½ teaspoon salt
¼ cup hot water
1 cup all-purpose flour

For the soup
2 tablespoons vegetable oil
1 medium yellow onion, finely chopped
1 carrot, peeled and grated
1 pound ground turkey
1 teaspoon dried Mexican oregano
1 teaspoon sweet paprika
1 garlic clove, minced
4 cups vegetable broth
½ cup chopped parsley
Salt, to taste
Pepper, to taste

1. **For the dough:** Dissolve the salt in the water. Add flour, working with a fork, and later your hands, to form a soft elastic dough. If it is too stiff, add more water 1 tablespoon at a time. Knead for 4 minutes. Cover.

2. **For the soup:** Heat 2 tablespoons of oil in a large pot over medium-high heat. Add the onion and carrots and cook 5 minutes, stirring occasionally

3. Add the turkey, oregano, paprika, garlic, salt, and pepper. Cook 6 minutes.

4. Add the broth and cover. When it begins to boil, reduce the heat to simmer.

5. Roll the dough to ⅛-inch, and cut into 1-inch squares.

6. Add the *pantrucas* to the boiling soup 4 to 6 at a time. They will sink and then resurface. Keep adding more each time the soup comes back to a boil, until they are all cooked.

7. Serve hot with parsley as garnish.

Note: If you have leftovers, store the dumplings separate from the soup or they may become gummy.

AJIACO | *Grilled Steak Soup*

SERVES 4

Three strong cultural factors converge to create this delicious grilled steak soup. The first is the weekend tradition of the asado *(barbecue) in Chile. The second is that any Chilean host would be horrified if the spread they put out were meager, so there are always plenty of leftovers. The third one is that we'll make soup out of pretty much anything that stands still.*

Leftover grilled meat is the basis of Chile's ajiaco, *a soup which shares its names with many other, very different soups across Latin America. Do not bring this soup to a boil, following the instructions of the older generation who would tell you that your pot was getting away from you (*se te está arrancando la olla*) if they came upon it bubbling furiously. A simmer is best.*

As a summer alternative, we might skip the soup-making and serve leftover barbecued meat as a salpicón *salad, where cubes of leftover grilled meat are tossed with lettuce, cooked carrots, boiled potatoes, tomatoes, or red pepper.*

1 pound grilled flank steak
1 medium yellow onion
2 tablespoons vegetable oil
1 medium carrot, sliced in
  ¼-inch thick rounds
½ red bell pepper, seeded and
  thinly sliced
½ teaspoon paprika
1 teaspoon hot sauce, optional
1 teaspoon dried Mexican
  oregano
4 cups beef broth
6 medium red potatoes, peeled
  and cut into wedges
Salt, to taste
Pepper, to taste
½ cup chopped parsley

1. Cut the meat into 2-inch-long strips.

2. Peel the onion, then cut lengthwise and slice thinly.

3. In a large pot, over medium-high heat, heat 2 tablespoons of oil and add the onion. Cook 5 minutes.

4. Add the carrot and bell pepper, and cook for 2 more minutes, stirring occasionally.

5. Add the paprika, hot sauce, and oregano. Add the broth, carrots, pepper, and potatoes, cover, and cook for 15 minutes.

6. Scoop out half of the potatoes and mash well, return them to the soup, and add the meat and any of its juices.

7. Adjust the seasoning with salt and pepper, and serve hot with parsley sprinkled on top.

POROTOS CON RIENDAS
Winter Bean Stew with Pasta
SERVES 4

This peculiarly-named dish (literally: beans with reins) comes to us straight from the campo *(countryside) where hearty meals are the norm. The starch of the beans combines perfectly with the starch released by the spaghetti, making this dish nice and thick. Unlike* Porotos Granados/Bean, Corn, and Squash Potage *(page 29), the summer bean potage, this dish uses the dried* tórtola *bean, which has a resilient skin and does not easily turn to mush.*

This dish is very forgiving — if you have a little more or a little less of most of the ingredients, it won't harm the final product. It's perfect for winter as it doesn't require any fussy seasonal vegetables, only squash and onions, which are available year-round. For many people it's a hardwired comfort food and delivers the kind of nostalgia you might associate with macaroni and cheese. Porotos con Riendas *is probably nearly as old as Chile itself, and remains a favorite among miners,* huasos *(cowboys) and your average office worker looking for a hearty, inexpensive meal that reminds them of home.*

2 tablespoons vegetable oil

1 medium yellow onion, diced

1 Spanish chorizo if available, or substitute mild kielbasa (14-oz.), in 1½-inch lengths

1 garlic clove, minced

1 teaspoon dried Mexican oregano

½ teaspoon ground cumin

Salt, to taste

1 teaspoon paprika

4 cups vegetable broth

2 cups cubed fresh or frozen butternut squash

8 oz. spaghetti

2 (15.5-oz.) cans pinto beans, rinsed

Color to serve (optional, see page 10)

1. In a large pot, over medium-high heat, heat 2 tablespoons oil, add the onion, and cook 5 minutes. Add the chorizo, garlic, oregano, cumin, salt, and paprika, and cook 1 minute.

2. Add the broth and the squash.

3. Once it comes to a boil again, add the spaghetti and the beans.

4. Cook 10 minutes until the pasta is cooked.

5. Serve hot with a teaspoon of *color*.

TORTILLA DE ZANAHORIA
Stove-Top Carrot Frittata
SERVES 6

It may surprise you, but many a Chilean cook wouldn't be caught in a kitchen without a box grater. So essential is this simple implement that it travels on vacation or to beach houses with some people, and you can even find one by default in rental homes on the beach or in the mountains. And one of the reasons is so that you can shred carrots, for salads, and for the unmissable tortilla de zanahoria, *or stove-top carrot frittata.*

Instead of being egg-focused, this frittata actually only uses eggs to hold the carrots—which are the star of the dish—together. This is a great dish to make sure everyone is getting their vegetables in the winter months, when salads fall out of favor in Chile. While fresh carrots (with tops attached) are usually the sweetest, whatever carrots you have on hand—even if a bit forgotten in the back of the fridge—can be used. Though cheese would never be present in a tortilla de verduras *(vegetable frittata), here we add a little dairy for creaminess.*

2 tablespoons vegetable oil, divided
1 medium yellow onion, diced
4 large carrots, peeled and grated
3 tablespoons parsley, chopped
2 eggs
2 tablespoons whole milk or whipping cream
Salt, to taste
Pepper, to taste

1. Heat an 8 or 10-inch cast-iron skillet over medium heat.

2. Add 1 tablespoon of oil and the onion to the skillet. Cook for 6 to 8 minutes, stirring occasionally until the onion starts to brown.

3. Move the onion to a bowl, and combine with the carrots and parsley.

4. In another bowl, place the eggs, milk or cream, salt, and pepper, and whisk vigorously for a few minutes. Pour this mixture on top of the carrots and mix.

5. In the same cast-iron skillet, over medium heat, heat the remaining oil. Pour in the carrot mixture and press down so the mixture is flat and fills the whole skillet.

6. Cook covered 10 to 12 minutes, until almost completely set.

7. Finish cooking it in the oven, broiling uncovered until brown on top, about 4 to 6 minutes. Remove from oven and allow it to cool for 5 minutes.

8. Invert it onto a serving plate or board to serve.

COLIFLOR EN SALSA NOGADA
Cauliflower with Walnut Sauce
SERVES 4

This is one of very few vegetable dishes in Chile that comes with a sauce. Cauliflower has four main presentations in Chile: in a type of giardiniera *salad we call* pickle *(say: peek LEH), as fritters, as part of a composed salad, or as a stand-alone dish with this creamy walnut sauce. The preparation dates back many generations, and for a long time people saw béchamel as a barometer of general cooking skill, and having a lumpy béchamel sauce was considered a total failure. Nowadays you can whip away any lumps in a blender, and anyway, we have faith in your whisking capabilities.*

Nutmeg is imported to Chile and was historically considered a bit of a luxury. This is one of the only savory dishes that uses it. Its use may be explained by the fact that béchamel sauce by itself doesn't have much flavor, and more than one chef has pointed out that the ingredients bear a striking resemblance to those for engrudo, *or wallpaper paste. But with the buttery base and adding the nutmeg, a delicious sauce is made. This dish pairs particularly well with* Papas Doradas/Golden Potatoes *(page 93).*

1 large or 2 medium heads of cauliflower
½ cup walnuts, chopped small
3 tablespoons unsalted butter
3 tablespoons all-purpose flour
2 cups whole milk
1 teaspoon salt
½ teaspoon pepper
½ teaspoon fresh grated nutmeg

1. Cut the cauliflower in small florets of equal size.

2. In a medium pot, boil 2 inches of salted water. Add the florets and cover. Cook for 4 minutes and taste, the cauliflower needs to be cooked but not soft. Cook up to 2 minutes more if required. Drain and set aside.

3. In the same pot or in a skillet, toast the walnuts over medium heat until fragrant. Let cool in a bowl.

4. In the same pot or in a skillet, melt the butter over medium heat, add the flour and cook, stirring continuously, for 2 minutes.

5. Remove from the heat and slowly add the milk, whisking continuously.

6. Return the sauce to the heat, add the walnuts, salt, pepper, and nutmeg, keep stirring, and allow the sauce to boil for 1 minute. It will thicken.

7. Taste the sauce and adjust the seasoning.

8. Pour the sauce over the cauliflower and serve.

PAPAS DORADAS | *Golden Potatoes*

SERVES 4

*Potatoes originated in South America, and were unknown in Europe and the rest of the world until the 1500s. Pablo Neruda, one of Chile's Nobel Prize–winning poets, wrote an ode to the potato in which he points out that the Quechua word that we use in South America (*papa*) is the original, not* patata, *as they use in Spain. It feels deeply rooted in the Chilean culture to eat potatoes, which we buy by the kilo or the woven sackful at the local market.*

Though there are some 200 native species of potato spread over the country's territory, including the blu-ish-purple potato from Chiloé, the most commonly used is a thin-skinned, red potato. They are used in Chile in soups and stews, and potatoes are a more popular side dish than rice or pasta, often boiled or as mashed potatoes. Here they are parboiled and then pan fried in a combination of oil and butter that allows for high temperatures that yield a beautiful crisp exterior and creamy, rich interior. This dish makes a great side for Coliflor en Salsa Nogada/*Cauliflower with Walnut Sauce (page 91) or* Tomaticán/*Juicy Summery Tomato and Meat Sauté (page 37).*

5 large red potatoes
2 teaspoons salt
2 tablespoons vegetable oil
1 tablespoon butter
¼ cup chopped flat parsley

1. Peel the potatoes and cut into cubes.

2. Fill a pot with water and add 2 teaspoons of salt. Add the potatoes, turn on the heat to medium-high, and cover. Once boiling, reduce the heat and cook for 10 minutes. Drain.

3. In a medium skillet, heat the oil and butter over medium-high heat. Add the potatoes in one layer and let cook without moving for 3 minutes, flip them, and keep cooking until all sides are golden.

4. Add the parsley and serve immediately.

CHUPE DE MARISCOS | *Baked Seafood Casserole*

SERVES 4

This cheesy baked casserole is part savory bread pudding, part seafood delight. The word chupe *comes from the Quechua, and was originally used to refer to a meat dish. The modern* chupe *is laced with and topped with cheese. It comes from the north of Chile but is popular throughout the country as a weekend restaurant meal or for Easter lunch.*

When this dish is made only with crab, as opposed to mixed seafood, it is called a pastel, *but the preparation is the same. We recognize that in the United States, mixed seafood is generally easier to source, but we love both dishes equally. Don't skimp on the paprika, which gives it a warm color in addition to adding flavor.*

1 pound seafood mix (calamari, shrimp, scallops, crawfish, etc.)
2 tablespoons vegetable oil
1 medium yellow onion, diced
1 garlic clove, minced
½ red bell pepper, diced finely
8 slices of bread, crusts removed
1 (12 fl. oz) can evaporated milk
1 tablespoon paprika
1 cup sauvignon blanc
1½ cups grated Parmesan cheese, divided
Salt, to taste
Pepper, to taste

1. If using frozen seafood mix, defrost first. Chop the pieces into bite-size cubes.

2. In a medium pot, over medium-high heat, add 2 tablespoons of oil. When hot, add the onion, garlic, and bell pepper. Cook, stirring occasionally, for 10 minutes.

3. In a bowl, mix the bread with the evaporated milk and use a fork to work it into a paste.

4. Add the paprika to the pot, followed by the wine, and cook 2 minutes to reduce.

5. Add the bread-milk paste, seafood, and 1 cup of cheese.

6. Mix vigorously, cook 3 minutes. Add salt and pepper to taste.

7. Transfer to a baking dish and top with the remaining cheese.

8. Broil to brown and serve.

COSTILLAR DE CHANCHO PICANTE
Spicy Pork Ribs

SERVES 6

We use the expression pasarlo chancho *to mean "have a great time," or literally "spend time like a pig." The idea here is that pigs have a great time lolling around and eating leftovers. As in English, in Chilean Spanish we also have* chanchear, *which means to pig out.*

Pigs are often slaughtered for festive meals, such as weddings, funerals, or baptisms. It's a nose-to-tail affair with headcheese, pigs' feet, and other delicacies, including chicharrones, *or pork cracklings. There's even a festival in the mid-southern city of Talca dedicated to the celebratory nature of eating pork, always held in winter, as that's when pork is generally eaten.*

One of the most prized cuts is the costillar, *or rack of ribs. Here they are cooked with a little bit of spice and a touch of vinegar so they come out tangy. If you're from the southern states or love grits, that's another traditional accompaniment in Chile (called* chuchoca). *Permission has officially been granted from the Chilean higher-ups. You may eat this one with your hands.*

2 tablespoons smoked paprika
1 tablespoon ground black
    pepper
1 teaspoon ground cumin
1 tablespoon dried Mexican
    oregano
5 garlic cloves, minced
3 tablespoons vegetable oil
2 tablespoons red wine vinegar
2 tablespoons hot sauce
1 tablespoon salt
Hot water
1 (3–4 pounds) rack St. Louis–
    style spare ribs

1. Mix all ingredients other than the ribs in the blender. Top off with enough water to make 1 cup of marinade.

2. Clean the ribs. Cut off any remaining membrane and split the rack in half.

3. Place the racks in a baking dish and cover with the marinade. Turn the racks a couple of times, so all of the meat comes in contact with the marinade.

4. Cover and refrigerate overnight.

5. Preheat the oven to 300°F.

6. Place the ribs on a baking sheet and cover with aluminum foil. Cook for 2 hours.

7. Uncover and keep cooking (30 minutes to 1 hour) until the meat loosens from the bone and the internal temperature is between 145 and 160°F.

8. Let rest for 10 minutes before cutting and serving.

LECHE NEVADA | *Meringue Clouds in Vanilla Custard*

SERVES 8

Milky and custardy desserts are very popular in Chile, and it would seem that the combinations and cooking methods are infinite. Milk and eggs are readily available and not overly expensive, making this dessert an easy choice. Leche nevada *is cooked on the stove top, and while it requires a bit more skill than* Leche Asada de Damascos/*Baked Milk and Apricot Pudding (page 23) or* Sémola con Leche/*Semolina Pudding (page 69), the payoff is great, both in flavor and appearance.*

The translation of leche nevada *as "snowy milk" refers to the floating puffs of meringue in the custard. The heated milk first cooks the meringues and then becomes the custard. The meringues puff up, and then shrink, but the cooking gives them a more cellular structure inside, and though they are not marshmallows, there's a certain undeniable pillowy marshmallowiness to them.*

Leche nevada can be served warm or cold, and you are more likely to be served this homey dessert at someone's house than to find it at a restaurant.

4 cups whole milk

4 eggs, whites and yolks separated

1 cup granulated sugar, divided

1 tablespoon cornstarch

1 tablespoon vanilla extract

2 teaspoons ground cinnamon

1. In a medium or large skillet warm the milk to a gentle simmer over medium heat.

2. Beat the egg whites until frothy, add ½ cup of sugar slowly, and keep beating until hard peaks form.

3. Scoop the meringue into the simmering milk, dropping in one scoop at a time, for a total of 16 meringues, in batches. Cook 1 minute each side. With a slotted spoon, move each "cloud" onto a plate.

4. Make a custard: In a medium bowl, beat the egg yolks with a balloon whisk for 30 seconds. Add the remaining ½ cup of sugar and the cornstarch. Whisk to mix fully.

5. Add 1 ladleful of milk in a small stream into the egg yolks, whisking continuously, to temper the eggs. Return the egg-yolk-and-milk mixture to the pot with the milk and cook this mixture until it thickens. Remove from the heat. Add the vanilla and mix.

6. Pour the vanilla custard into a baking dish, and top with the meringue clouds.

7. Dust with cinnamon just before serving.

8. Serve warm or cold. Keep refrigerated.

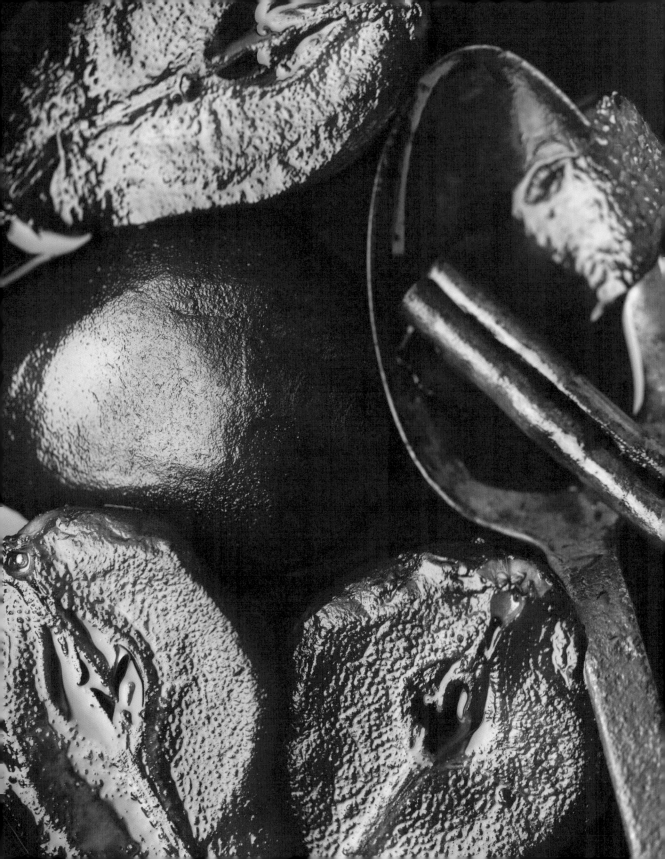

PERAS CON VINO | *Pears Poached in Red Wine*

SERVES 4

This dessert is considered elegant by some, though it is of no higher pedigree than many of the other desserts with European roots we eat in Chile. It joins together two ingredients that we routinely enjoy in Chile, which are fresh fruit and wine. Further, Chile is responsible for the production of some 10 percent of the world's pears, and is the world's fifth largest exporter of red wine, so this pairing seems completely natural and not at all fussy to us. Though there is no doubt that the velvety, purple surface of the pears contrasts beautifully with the creamy white of the interior and is a bit of a showstopper.

Peras con vino may remind you of the soft apple desserts you know, but pears and apples in fact cook up quite differently. Apples easily lose their structure, whereas pears stand tall. As the expression goes, you can't comparar peras con manzanas (literally, you can't compare pears with apples, though the expression in English is of course about apples and oranges).

2 cups red wine
½ cup granulated sugar
2 inches orange peel
3 whole cloves
1 (3-inch) cinnamon stick
4 firm green pears

1. In a medium skillet over medium-high heat, add the wine, sugar, orange peel, cloves, and cinnamon. Mix and allow to come to a boil, then lower the heat to a simmer.

2. Peel the pears, carefully leaving the stems intact. Cut in half lengthwise.

3. Add the pears to the simmering wine cut-side down and cook covered for 10 minutes. Flip them over and cook them an additional 5 to 10 minutes, until they are easily pierced with a table knife.

4. Remove the pears to a plate.

5. Keep cooking the wine until it thickens and reduce it to a syrup, about 10 minutes. Remove the cinnamon and orange peel.

6. Serve warm or cold with the syrup.

AGÜITAS DE YERBAS | *Herbal Tea*

SERVES 1

In the United States, people relegate herbal tea to when they are feeling unwell. In Chile, however, hosts offer herbal tea as part of the tea-coffee-tisane trifecta, particularly after dinner, as a bajativo *or* digestif. *Because we do not generally have central heat in Chile, a cup of herbal tea acts as a portable heater, both in hand and from the inside out.*

Many Chileans have aromatics growing outside for making herbal tea and also to repel mosquitoes. One popular plant is rue, which is said to keep evil out of homes and businesses when placed by the left side of the door. Pro tip: tie a red ribbon around one stalk or the flowerpot itself for extra protection.

For those who don't grow herbs, dried will do, and in Chile, these are available in supermarkets, and from enterprising yerberos *(herb-sellers) that set up their tables outside of hospitals and clinics. Lemon peel makes a great tisane as well. So great is our love for herbal tea in Chile that we can even make an* agüita *with nothing in it, serving boiled water as* agua perra, *a name of unknown etymology.*

2-inch sprig Greek or Mexican oregano, lemon verbena, mint, or lemon peel

Sugar or multifloral honey or *miel de ulmo* (see Pantry, page 10)

1. In a mug or cup, place your herb of choice.

2. Cover with boiling water and let steep 2 minutes. Remove the herbs.

3. Add sugar or honey as desired.

Spring

After watching the sunlight wane, and bundling up through the coldest months of winter, it is with great celebration that we flip the calendar from August to September. At the beginning of September, it seems all of Chile throws their windows open to receive the first rays of spring light and warmth. Though spring officially begins on September 21st, it is commonly accepted that September 1st is the beginning of spring in Chile.

September brings brisk breezes that lift colorful kites into the sky, and everyone begins to get ready for Chile's Fiestas Patrias (national holidays) on the 18th and 19th of the month. So central is this event to the Chilean identity that we abbreviate the whole celebration, calling it *el dieciocho*, the number eighteen in Spanish. And so widespread is the celebration that you'd be hard-pressed to find a store, apartment building, private home, or taxi that wasn't flying at least one Chilean flag.

To get a picture of the 18th celebrations, think of it as a countrywide county fair. Everything other than holiday festivities grinds to a complete halt, and everyone takes a few days to celebrate, including eating all of the traditional foods that go with this season. September smells like cooking meat over charcoal, which you can easily trace to the sizzling *anticuchos* (kebabs) on many a grill. Then there's the smell of hot sauce squirted on *choripanes* (sausage rolls) and empanadas, and the sweet carnival smells of candied peanuts and cotton candy.

Many Chileans break out their best *huaso* (cowboy-style) gear for dancing the *cueca* (the national dance) which is a hat tip to the mating dance between a rooster and a hen, and can be seen everywhere from traffic lights to office parties and at *fondas*, the large public parties that commemorate the beginning of Chile's independence process.

Primavera, which is the Spanish word for spring, seems to fly by. It calls forward to the next coming season of *verano*, or summer, when the year comes to a close and once again we can enjoy lazy days and free time with our friends and families.

Spring

PISCO SOUR CON CEDRÓN
Lemon Verbena Pisco Sour
SERVES 6

Pisco is a distilled grape brandy, and pisco sour is one of the drinks to which Chileans hold most firmly. There is a local pride in Chilean pisco production, which by law takes place in the north of Chile and is strictly regulated. Peru also produces pisco, and this is a topic it's best not to get Chileans and Peruvians started on.

Traditionally, Chileans drank pisco sours as an aperitivo, *before a restaurant meal. Now, however, with a renewed interest in and love for Chilean flavors, and the rise of cocktail culture in Chile, people are also preparing them at home. At an informal gathering, guests may be asked to squeeze the lemons, which can be regular yellow lemons, or a smaller, more tart, green lemon we call* limón sutil, *or an even smaller one called* limón de pica, *both of which are more similar in taste to a lime.*

It is fashionable now to add different syrups and macerated herbs to give the pisco sour a special punch. We're big fans of lemon verbena, as you can see in the Agüitas de Yerbas/Herbal Tea *recipe on page 103, but you can use ginger or other fruity flavors, too. Our pisco sour has one raw egg white in it, because the foam on top is an important element. You can use pasteurized eggs if you prefer.*

12 lemon verbena leaves, stems removed
1 cup boiling water
1 cup granulated sugar
1 cup pisco
1 cup lemon juice
1 cup ice cubes
1 egg white
6 small lemon verbena sprigs, to garnish

1. Place the lemon verbena leaves in a mug, and pour boiling water over to cover. Let it steep 5 minutes.

2. Drain the lemon verbena water into a small pot and add the sugar. Heat over medium-high heat, stirring until the sugar dissolves. Remove from the heat before it boils. Let cool and refrigerate for up to 5 days.

3. In a blender, add the pisco, lemon juice, lemon verbena syrup, ice, and egg white. Blend until frothy.

4. Serve in coupe glasses and garnish with the lemon verbena sprigs.

5. Serve immediately.

TERREMOTO | *Earthquake Cocktail*

SERVES 1

Traditionally this drink is based on pipeño, *a short-fermented, unfiltered wine. It's tangy and unfinished, and is slightly fizzy. The genesis of the name (and perhaps the drink) is that some German reporters who came to Chile after a large earthquake in 1985 suggested adding the pineapple sorbet to* pipeño *and declared "now that's an earthquake."*

The short history of this drink makes it no less Chilean, and it's commonly drunk during el dieciocho, *the national holiday celebrated in September. Also, sweet alcoholic drinks are very common in Chile, whether that's a pisco sour, a* vaina, Cola de Mono/Coffee Eggnog *(see page 181), or here, the beloved* terremoto. *Secondly, it's not that far afield of "ponche a la romana," which is what we call the Christmas and New Years' traditional drink of champagne with pineapple sorbet.*

Thirdly, and this requires a deep dive into the Chilean psyche, earthquakes are a part of the culture. Even years later, people still recount their experiences in the 2010 earthquake that measured 8.8 on the Richter scale in the central-south of Chile. The resilience of the Chilean people and infrastructure is a point of pride. Additional, smaller cups of the same terremoto *are, perhaps predictably, referred to as* réplicas *(aftershocks).*

½ ounce grenadine syrup
1 cup cold prosecco
1 cup chilled white wine
3 tablespoons pineapple sorbet

1. Pour the grenadine into a tumbler. Follow it with the prosecco and the wine, and top it with sorbet.

2. Serve immediately with a straw.

EMPANADAS DE PINO | *Beef Empanadas*

MAKES 10

So quintessential is the empanada to Chileans that upon visiting Chile, you are likely to be asked, "te gusta la comida chilena, te gustan las empanadas?" (Do you like Chilean food, do you like empanadas?) They are a staple of the national holiday in September, but are eaten year-round, and for many families these are a traditional Sunday meal or a starter before a lunch.

Though many Latin American countries have empanadas, they each have different doughs and fillings. Chile's empanada dough is wheat-based, and the traditional filling always contains pino *(ground beef cooked with onions and cumin). Hard-boiled eggs, olives, and raisins are found throughout, though by request of picky eaters, some cooks will make a few without this or that, depending on taste.*

Traditionally, empanadas were baked in a community oven, and people used distinctive patterns of folding and crimping so they could identify and take home their own. The proper way to eat an empanada is to hold it upright, break off the top cachito *of dough and eat it first, using that time to let the empanada vent some of its steam. If it drips down your arm, well, that's just part of the experience.*

For the filling
2 tablespoons vegetable oil
1 pound ground beef
½ cup beef or vegetable broth
1 tablespoon paprika
½ teaspoon ground cumin
Salt, to taste
Pepper, to taste
2 medium yellow onions, chopped
1 tablespoon all-purpose flour

For the dough
1 cup whole milk, warm
½ tablespoon salt
4½ cups all-purpose flour
1 egg
6 tablespoons lard or butter, melted and warm

To assemble
20 raisins
10 black olives, pitted
3 eggs, hard-boiled
1 beaten egg to seal and brush

1. **Make the meat filling:** In a large pot or skillet, warm 2 tablespoons of oil over medium-high heat.

2. Add the meat and cook 4 minutes, without breaking it apart. Flip it over, and cook 4 more minutes. Break it apart and add the broth, paprika, cumin, salt, and pepper. Lower the heat to medium. Cook 10 minutes.

3. Add the onions and cook 30 minutes.

4. Add flour and mix well. Remove from the heat and let cool. Refrigerate overnight.

5. **Make the dough:** Mix the milk with the salt until dissolved.

6. Use a food processor, or a stand mixer, to blend the flour, egg, and lard until it resembles coarse crumbs. With the machine running on low speed, add the milk in a stream.

7. The dough should be soft. If necessary, add warm water by the tablespoon until it softens.

8. Knead for 5 minutes.

9. Preheat the oven to 350°F.

10. Transfer the dough to a floured counter and split into 10 equal portions.

11. For each empanada, flatten a ball of dough with your palm and roll it into an 8-inch circle.

12. Place 3 tablespoons of meat filling, 2 raisins, 1 whole olive, and ¼ of a hard-boiled egg on the bottom half of the dough, avoiding the edge.

13. Wet the edge of the dough with egg and seal it shut, pressing down all around the seam. Fold the seam 3 times, sealing the curved part first, and then forming what will be the *cachitos* (horns) of the empanada. Brush each empanada with egg, and using a toothpick make 3 holes in the top of each one to allow the steam to escape.

14. Bake for 35 minutes or until golden.

15. Serve hot.

ANTICUCHOS | *Beef and Pork Skewers*

SERVES 8

Not every day has enough time for the ceremony that is the Chilean asado *(barbecue).* Asados *are time-consuming affairs, between piling up the charcoal and waiting for it to light, the fire to spread, and the meat to cook over a slow fire. Sometimes you want the taste of the grill, but a little less effort. For that, the* anticucho *(skewered meat) is perfect.*

But make no mistake, these grilled meat skewers are still a cause for celebration, and are popular for the September national holiday and birthdays alike. In Chile they are a mixed skewer, with beef, pork, and sausage all sharing space. They're portable, more economical than grilling large cuts of meat, and more forgiving in inclement weather. And it wouldn't be a Chilean anticucho *if you didn't marinate the meat in a vinegar-oregano-paprika* adobo *and pierce a piece of freshly grilled bread on the end of the metal skewer before handing it over to a hungry guest.*

1 pound blade steak pork or loin
1 pound New York strip beef or
    top sirloin
½ cup wine vinegar
1 teaspoon dried Mexican
    oregano
1 teaspoon paprika
Salt, to taste
Pepper, to taste
1 yellow onion
1 red bell pepper
1 mild kielbasa sausage
Baguette, to serve, cut in 3-inch
    lengths
Metal skewers

1. Cut the meat into 2-inch cubes. Place in a bowl.

2. To prepare the marinade, combine the vinegar, oregano, paprika, salt, and pepper. Pour over the meat and mix. Cover and let rest for 3 hours in the fridge.

3. Preheat the grill to high.

4. Cut the onion and bell pepper into 1-inch squares.

5. Cut the kielbasa into 2-inch-long pieces.

6. Skewer alternating meat, sausage, onion, bell pepper.

7. Grill 5 minutes on one side, flip, and cook 5 additional minutes.

8. Before serving, push a piece of baguette onto the end of the skewer.

APIO CON PALTA | *Avocado Celery Salad*

SERVES 4

In the United States, raw celery is often relegated to iterations of ants on a log (celery spread with cream cheese or peanut butter and raisins), as an accompaniment to carrots on a crudité plate, or standing tall in a Bloody Mary. Not so in Chile, where it grows incredibly well (to Gilligan's Island–type proportions), and it is the backbone of one of Chile's favorite salads.

Apio con Palta is fresh and bright and perfect as an accompaniment to stew or other soft foods, giving that crunch that is essential to every meal. It's also one of the elemental salads of a Chilean barbecue, and it's one of the only times you'll see avocado cubed in Chile, as opposed to mashed.

Don't skip the olives and/or radishes, which give a nice color and flavor contrast. It is important for this and every salad served in a home in Chile is that it's dressed in the kitchen, not on people's plates. Every kitchen has a command center where the oil, vinegar, salt, and pepper take up residence, and unless you're at a restaurant, you'd seldom see dressings on the table. Feel free to use white wine vinegar if your family prefers it over lemon.

1 bunch celery
2 radishes
2 large avocados
3 lemons, juiced
2 tablespoons vegetable oil
½ cup pitted black olives or walnuts (we use *aceitunas de Azapa*)
Salt, to taste

1. Use a potato peeler to gently remove the outer layer of the heartier celery ribs. Cut into bite-sized pieces. Leave a couple of leaves in the mix.

2. Cut the radishes into thin slices.

3. Soak the celery and radishes in ice water for 2 hours. Drain.

4. Cut the avocado into bite-sized pieces.

5. Mix everything in a bowl. Dress with the lemon juice, and 2 tablespoons of oil, sprinkle with olives or walnuts, and season with salt.

CREMA DE BERROS | *Watercress Soup*

SERVES 4

Watercress, though not that commonly eaten in the United States, with the possible exception of on tea sandwiches, is very popular in Chile. As a salad, we dress it with lemon or vinegar, but in times before regulations ensured vegetables were irrigated with clean water, Chileans turned to making watercress into soup as a way to keep on eating this fresh, tasty green.

Before going on, we have to mention that there are two main types of soup in Chile—brothy and pureed—and that we call them by different names. Pureed soups are not called sopas, *but instead are referred to as* cremas. *While these could theoretically be topped with cream in Chile, the puree is made of vegetables—here we use watercress, but you could easily substitute baby spinach—and made with potatoes to give the soup body and creaminess. In fact, in Chile, we make pureed soups out of almost every vegetable, but curiously, never tomato, which is so popular in the United States.*

Though this soup is refreshing and light, it would only ever be served hot in Chile, often as a starter. This is a prime example of a food that tastes great topped with Salsa Verde/Parsley-Onion Salsa *(page 53).*

8 oz. watercress, tough stems removed
1 tablespoon vegetable oil
1 medium onion, diced
3 medium potatoes, peeled and cubed
4 cups vegetable broth
Salt, to taste
Pepper, to taste

1. Wash the watercress thoroughly.

2. In a large pot, warm 1 tablespoon of oil over medium heat. Add the onion and cook for 6 to 8 minutes, until soft.

3. Add the watercress, potatoes, and broth. Season with salt and pepper. Cook, covered, for 5 minutes.

4. Mix and lower the heat to a simmer. Cook for 15 minutes. Remove from heat.

5. Working in batches in a blender or with a stick blender, process until smooth.

6. Heat and adjust the seasoning.

7. Serve hot.

CAZUELA DE PAVA CON CHUCHOCA
Turkey Soup with Cornmeal
SERVES 4

We wish we knew why we say we make this hearty homemade soup, the dream meal of Chileans the world over, with pava, or she-turkey. For Christmas, we talk about the male pavo and here it's the pava. We have not yet found an explanation.

What we do know is that it is a deliciously traditional soup, for which every Chilean chef has their own recipe. Cazuela (which can be made with another meat, such as osso buco or chicken quarters if you prefer) is an important cultural institution, and a celebration of the return of fresh vegetables after a long winter. While winter soups tend to be in earth tones, here the splashes of yellow, green, and red portend the bounty that spring and summer bring. It's a true locavore treat, easily made from garden-fresh veggies, which are the heart and soul of this soup. Note that the fresh corn in the United States is too sweet for this dish, so we use frozen corn.

As a one-pot meal, cazuela can't be beat. And the use of cornmeal to give the stock a little extra umph reminds us of some thickened soups from the southwestern United States and Mexico.

1 tablespoon vegetable oil
4 small turkey drumsticks
Salt, to taste
Pepper, to taste
1 teaspoon ground cumin
1 yellow onion, diced
2 carrots, grated
½ red bell pepper, diced
3 garlic cloves, minced
4 medium red potatoes, peeled
4 ears frozen corn on the cob
1 small bunch parsley
¼ cup coarse stone-ground cornmeal
1 cup frozen French-cut green beans

1. In a large pot, warm 1 tablespoon of oil over medium-high heat.

2. Pat the turkey dry with a paper towel and season with salt, pepper, and the cumin. Sear 3 minutes each side and remove to a plate.

3. Add the onion, carrots, and bell pepper to the pot and cook for 6 minutes.

4. Add the garlic, turkey, potatoes, corn, and parsley into the pot. Cover with 8 cups of boiling water and place on high heat.

5. Once the soup comes back to a boil, lower the heat to keep it simmering. Cook, covered, for 15 minutes. Remove any foam that collects on top with a slotted spoon.

6. Add the cornmeal and green beans, and cook for 5 additional minutes. Adjust the seasoning.

7. Serve 1 turkey leg, one potato, one ear of corn, and plenty of soup in each bowl.

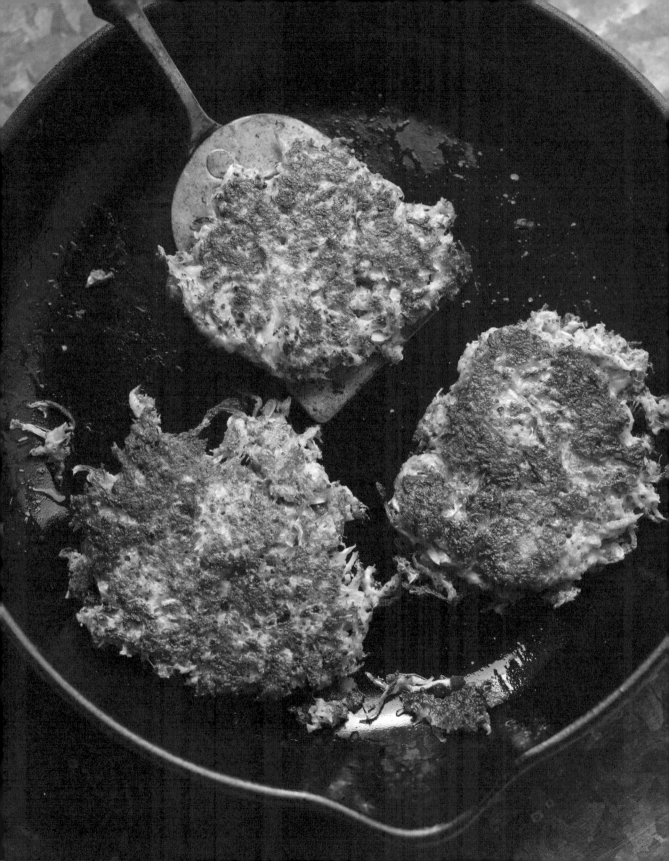

FRITOS DE BRÓCOLI | *Broccoli Fritters*
SERVES 4

If making a tortilla (skillet frittata) seems too daunting, particularly the flipping, which can take a bit of practice, start with this simple Chilean vegetable fritter recipe. We make it here with finely shredded broccoli, but cauliflower, green beans, carrots, zucchini, swiss chard or spinach, corn, or anything that is small or easily chopped is fair game. The cheese holds it together and pleases many palates. This dish can easily be made in advance and reheated in the microwave or oven, and is also good at room temperature. Due to its shape and resiliency, it seems natural that fritos could also stand in for a veggie burger, though Chileans would be unlikely to go there.

4 cups grated broccoli (a food processor would be great for this, or buy it pre-grated)
2 eggs, lightly beaten
½ cup all-purpose flour
½ cup mozzarella cheese, grated
Salt, to taste
Pepper, to tastee
3 tablespoons vegetable oil

1. Discard any liquid from the grated broccoli.
2. In a bowl, combine the broccoli, eggs, flour, and cheese. Season with salt and pepper.
3. Warm 3 tablespoons of oil in a medium skillet over medium-high heat.
4. Scoop ¼ cup of the broccoli mixture into the skillet and press down gently with the back of a spoon to form a patty. Repeat with the rest of the mixture, without crowding the pan. Add more oil if necessary.
5. Cook 3 minutes on each side.
6. Remove with a spatula and drain on paper towels.
7. Serve hot or at room temperature.

SALMON CANCATO

Salmon Stuffed with Sausage, Tomato, and Cheese

SERVES 4

This recipe comes to us from the south of Chile, tracing its etymology to Mapundungún, the language of the indigenous Mapuche people. Cancay means to grill or to toast. Originally, cancato was made with róbalo (similar to branzino) or sierra (mackerel is a close substitute), and cooked on a spit, or secured with baling wire and grilled. Nowadays we make it with salmon, and this oven-based version is much more common.

Eating salmon together with tomatoes, sausage, and cheese may sound curious, but the sausage lends a smoky taste, and the creamy cheese blends those two flavors. The tomatoes soften and their juices help keep everything moist. And the salmon is there to soak up all the flavors of these three ingredients. The combination is delectable. We show it here with a half salmon, because in Chile we use the whole fish, but we have reworked the recipe for a weeknight dinner using fillets.

1 yellow onion

1 tablespoon vegetable oil

Salt, to taste

Pepper, to taste

2 teaspoons dried Mexican oregano, divided

4 (4-oz.) salmon fillets, deboned

1 mild uncured kielbasa, ½-inch slices

2 tomatoes, ½-inch slices

6 slices Havarti cheese

1. Preheat the oven to 450°F.

2. Peel and halve the onion lengthwise, and slice thinly.

3. Grease a baking dish with vegetable oil, add the onion, and season with salt, pepper, and half the oregano.

4. Lay the salmon on top of the onions, and season with salt and pepper. Add the kielbasa and then the tomatoes. Cover the dish with aluminum foil.

5. Bake 15 minutes. Uncover and place the cheese on top of the tomatoes and sprinkle the remaining oregano on top.

6. Bake 5 minutes. Check the salmon—it is cooked when it flakes easily.

7. Serve hot.

CHARQUICÁN | *Potato-Squash Stew with Beef*

SERVES 4

What if there were a dish that had all of your cupboard and kitchen staples, was warm, hearty, nutritious, inexpensive, quick to make, and had all the flavors of home? You'd make it frequently. In Chile that dish is charquicán. *The origin of the name lays in the word* charqui, *which is where the English word "jerky" comes from, but this dish is made with fresh meat. In summertime, when tomatoes are at their best, some chefs add tomatoes to the* sofrito, *the sauteéd aromatics that start a dish.*

Charquicán is a big favorite among many Chileans, which is handy, because the main ingredients are generally available. It's easy to make vegetarian, and the sunny-side-up egg on top (never over easy in Chile) is the finishing touch that brings the plate together.

This stew traces its history to the sixteenth century, and versions of it can be found in Chile's three bordering countries, Argentina, Peru, and Bolivia. It also appears in the episode of Anthony Bourdain's No Reservations *in which he came to Chile.*

1 tablespoon vegetable oil
1 small yellow onion, diced
1 pound ground beef
2 cups frozen butternut squash, cubed
4 medium red potatoes, peeled and cubed
1 teaspoon ground paprika
1 cup low sodium beef or vegetable broth
1 cup frozen corn
½ cup frozen peas or chopped green beans
Salt, to taste
Pepper, to taste

1. In a large pot, warm 1 tablespoon of oil over medium-high heat.

2. Add the onion and cook until soft, 6 to 8 minutes.

3. Push the onion to the side and add the beef, cook 3 minutes, stir, and cook for 3 more minutes. Season to taste.

4. Add the squash, potatoes, paprika, and the broth. Mix. Cover and cook for 15 minutes.

5. Lower the heat and use a potato masher to partially mash the potatoes and squash, leaving some chunks.

6. Add the corn and peas or green beans and cook for 4 minutes more until everything is heated through.

7. Adjust the seasoning and serve with a fried egg or *color* (see Pantry, page 10).

TURRÓN DE VINO | *Wine-Infused Swiss Meringue*

SERVES 8

This melt-in-your-mouth dessert is a great use for a small amount of red wine left over from the day before, or you could sneak a little out of today's wine without too much fuss. The pale purple color is a lovely touch at the end of the meal, and the sweet, pillowy meringue is a big favorite among all ages.

The word turrón *is used in Spanish to mean many things, from a nearly jaw-breaking hard Spanish nougat to a softer nougat, to here, which is a Swiss meringue. Traditionally,* Turrón de Vino *was made by slowly streaming a hot syrup into partially beaten egg whites, but this version, in addition to being easier to handle, is also fridge-stable for a day at least, whereas the traditional version would hold for a couple of hours at most.*

Beating the turrón *is an important step. It's somewhat time-consuming, but watching the meringue ruffle and swirl in the bowl as the beaters go is mesmerizing. You could also read a book or grab your phone, and the* turrón *will not suffer.*

4 egg whites
1 cup granulated sugar
½ cup cabernet sauvignon
½ cup chopped walnuts or
    pecans (optional)

1. Use a large double boiler, or a large pot with 2 inches of water in it, and a metal bowl set inside so that it is supported by the edges of the pot but does not touch the water below. Heat the water to boil and then lower the heat to simmer.

2. In the bowl mix the egg whites, sugar, and wine. With a handheld mixer, beat slowly until the sugar dissolves.

3. Turn the speed to high and beat until a glossy meringue with hard peaks develops, about 8 minutes.

4. Carefully remove the bowl from the pot and keep beating the meringue at high speed until it cools down.

5. Add the optional walnuts or pecans on top just before serving.

MOTE CON HUESILLOS
Sweetened Dried Peach Punch with Barley
SERVES 4

A cross between a drink and a snack (or perhaps a drinkable snack), Mote con Huesillos *is the go-to summer refreshment in plazas around Chile. It is served from carts and stands, and very few people would make it at home, as it is readily available in the warmer months.*

The word mote *refers to wheatberries, though here we substitute the nearly indistinguishable cooked barley, and* huesillos *(literally little bones) refers to the dried peaches, which in Chile come dried on the pit. The juice is made by reconstituting the dried peaches in water with sugar and spices, and when served, the glass is usually ⅓ mote and one or two peach halves, and the rest is juice. It is always served with a spoon, which you can (and should) use to scoop out the peaches and the grain.*

You can vary the proportions of grain, peaches, and juice in the final product to suit your tastes, but it would be an unpardonable sin to serve it at any temperature other than freezing cold, though it is never served over ice.

8 dried peach halves
4 cups water
1 (3-inch) cinnamon stick
2 inches orange peel
1 cup granulated sugar
2 cups cooked barley

1. Soak the peaches in the water overnight with the cinnamon and orange peel.

2. Put the peaches and soaking water in a medium pot. Cook for 15 to 20 minutes, until soft.

3. Add the sugar and mix until it dissolves. Let it cool. Refrigerate.

4. To serve, in a tumbler scoop ½ cup of barley (for barley cooking instructions, see page 61), 2 peach halves, and enough liquid to almost fill the glass.

5. Serve cold.

Once

If all of Chilean food is seasonal, there is one meal that transcends every time of year, and that most Chileans eat every day. And that meal is *once* (said: OHN-seh, like the number eleven in Spanish). Think of it as a teatime (and actually, some upper-class Chileans do refer to it as *té*). It is often the last meal of the day. There is no doubt that Chileans have a love affair with bread, and many people will stop by corner stores advertising that there's warm bread for people to buy on the way home from work. This fresh bread fulfills its destiny at the table for *once*.

Once, while universal, is as individual as the culture of every family. It is also highly regional, and might be more elaborate if it's a Sunday, someone's birthday, or guests are coming over. While you can eat *once* at a restaurant, it is generally thought to be better eaten at home, and is oftentimes the first meal you'd be invited to at someone else's house. Being invited over for *once* is a social indication of you being not just a casual acquaintance but someone your Chilean friends would actually like to (literally) break bread with.

Unlike most other meals, which are plated in the kitchen and brought to each diner, *once* is highly individual. Each person at the table chooses if they are feeling more salty or sweet that day, and how much they'd like to eat. In most homes in Chile, *quesillo* or *queso fresco*, a soft curdled cheese, is on the table, as well as jam, bread, avocado, and sandwich meats, and usually one mild, dessert-like food, like Bundt cake. Some families prefer to eat *once-comida*, which includes leftovers from that day's lunch. Depending on the family, *once* is eaten any time from about 6:00 p.m. to 10:00 p.m.

Drinking something warm, whether coffee, tea, or herbal tea, is an essential part of a grownup's *once*. The kettle is often boiled multiple times, between arriving shifts of people as household members check in at the end of the day. Children are usually given milk blended with the fruit in season, in the form of *leche con plátano* or *leche con frutillas* (see *Leche con Frutillas*/Strawberry Smoothie on page 151). And while the food is an important part of *tomando once* (eating once), the conversation over the kitchen table plays just as important a role.

Once

DULCE DE CAMOTE | *Sweet Potato Butter*

MAKES 3 CUPS

Most Chileans wouldn't dream of using sweet potatoes as the savory part of a meal, and would only use them to make camotillos, *which are little crescent-shaped sweets with a hard, sugary crust and a smooth, creamy interior.*

   Camotillos *are relatively easy to make in Chile, with a Japanese sweet potato that is yellow and fibrous on the inside. But the sweet potatoes available in the United States may be a different variety, with a smoother texture and a brighter color. The difference in sweet potato and the long drying time of* camotillos *makes them onerous to make in the United States. Here we present the solution, reimagining this treat as a soft fall-flavored puree enriched—as is the original—with orange zest. We recommend eating it garnished with cream or spread on toast as you would apple butter. It would also make a fantastic filling for a sponge cake or to replace the dulce de leche in the* Brazo de Reina/Dulce de Leche Swiss Roll *(page 175). Its beautiful orange color will have many a guest (incorrectly) guessing what the secret ingredient is.*

2 large sweet potatoes
2 cups granulated sugar
Zest of 1 orange

1. Preheat the oven to 350°F.

2. Pierce the sweet potatoes with a fork 8 times all around. Place on a baking sheet and bake for an hour and 15 minutes or until they can be easily pierced with a butter knife.

3. Remove from the oven and allow them to cool.

4. Peel the cooked sweet potatoes and puree them in the food processor. Scoop them into a medium pot and add the sugar and the orange zest.

5. Cook over medium heat until the mixture begins to bubble. Lower the heat and let the mixture reduce, stirring frequently, for 20 minutes. Be careful, as it can splatter.

6. Allow to cool to room temperature and serve as a dessert with whipped cream or use as you would apple butter. Refrigerated, it keeps 10 days.

CHURRASCA | *Quick Skillet Bread*

SERVES 6

Chileans eat a lot of bread, and often have a panera *(bread basket) on the table at mealtimes. While some breads are usually store bought, like our beloved version of French bread, the* marraqueta, *we also have a place for simpler fare. One of the best breads we know for beginners to try their hand at is the* churrasca, *a grilled savory quick (unyeasted) bread often eaten as a snack. Traditionally it would be made over coals in a steel drum with a grill on top or in a clay oven.*

Churrascas might look like pita at first blush, but they can't really be split open, so maybe think of them as a stiffer, smaller naan. You could top them with avocado for a more homemade version of avocado toast, though when eaten in the countryside in Chile, they come hot off the grill from able cooks' hands, and are nearly always served with butter.

A word to beginning Spanish speakers who occasionally mix up the -o and -a endings in Spanish: This is a place where the gender of the word really matters. A churrasco *is a giant meaty sandwich, and a chur-rasca is this delicious, fresh-cooked griddle bread.*

4 cups all-purpose flour
1½ teaspoons salt
½ teaspoon baking soda
½ teaspoon baking powder
¾ cup warm water
½ cup vegetable oil

1. Mix the flour, salt, baking soda, and baking powder in a bowl.

2. Combine the water and oil in a glass measuring cup.

3. Pour the oil-and-water mixture into the flour. Mix with a wooden spoon, and then use your hands to form a dough.

4. Knead for 10 minutes by hand or for 5 minutes in the mixer.

5. Split the dough into 6 equal parts. Roll each into a ball, flatten it by hand, and then roll with a rolling pin until they are ¼-inch thick.

6. Cook on an open grill set to medium-low heat or indirect heat for 5 minutes each side.

7. *Churrascas* can also be cooked on an iron skillet over medium-low heat for 5 minutes each side.

HUEVOS CON TOMATE
Scrambled Eggs with Tomatoes
SERVES 4

Much of the time, even in people's homes in Chile, eggs are served out of a small, single-serving double-handled aluminum dish called a paila, *and each person gets their own. But because* huevos con tomate *requires that you cook off much of the tomatoes' liquid before adding the egg, this dish is easier to make and serve out of a communal pan. Each person serves themselves directly from the skillet and onto their bread, bypassing their plate, to keep the eggs from cooling off before we take a bite.*

This is a great breakfast or once *when tomatoes are at their peak, and if you can get farm-fresh eggs, so much the better. Be careful not to overmix this dish. The result should be multihued; we would normally see the colors of both the white and the yolk. Also don't overcook; it, you want your eggs to commune with the bread, not just sit on top. Lastly, set your cast iron aside for* huevos con tomate, *unless it's enameled. The tomatoes will react with the cooking surface.*

3 beefsteak tomatoes
1 tablespoon vegetable oil
1 garlic clove, minced
5 eggs
Salt, to taste
Toasted bread, to serve

1. Dice the tomatoes, removing the seeds if you like.

2. In a nonreactive skillet, warm 1 tablespoon of oil, add the tomatoes and the garlic, and cook over medium heat until the juices have evaporated, approximately 5 to 8 minutes.

3. Add the eggs, folding them into the tomatoes. Season with salt. Remove from the heat before the eggs are completely cooked (they will continue to cook in the skillet).

4. Serve with bread.

DULCE DE ALCAYOTA | *Spaghetti Squash Preserves*

YIELDS 4 (8-OZ.) JARS

Alcayota is a curious vegetable, somewhere between a squash and a melon. It is about the size of a small watermelon, oblong and with a textured skin, with stripes that emanate from the vine end. When it comes to jam making, unlike other fruit, like berries, the alcayota (easily replaced with spaghetti squash for nearly identical results) is patient, and can wait until you are good and ready to make this sweet confection. It's ideal to make alcayota jam as the days grow cooler, and the emanating smell of caramel will bring everyone into the kitchen for "just a taste."

Once cooled, we like it scooped out onto bread at once or for breakfast, or served with panqueques (crepes). The jam has a mild flavor and is a textural treat, fresh and crunchy, while the syrup is reminiscent of honey.

1 (2–3 pound) spaghetti squash
About 1 pound granulated sugar
Zest of 1 orange
3 whole cloves

1. Preheat the oven to 400°F.
2. Pierce the squash and bake for 45 minutes. Allow it to cool.
3. Split it open, and remove the seeds. Scoop the pulp into a large bowl and weigh it.
4. This recipe assumes 2 pounds of squash. Add half the weight of the squash in sugar and stir well.
5. Let stand 12 hours or overnight. Don't skip this step; it is vital for the final texture of the jam.
6. The next day, cook over low heat. Let simmer for 20 minutes, stirring frequently.
7. Add the orange zest and cloves.
8. Stir well and continue to cook for an additional 25 minutes. If all of the liquid boils away, add up to a cup of water and cook for an additional 5 minutes. Allow to cool before serving. Keep refrigerated.
9. Serve with bread or crepes.

PAN CON PALTA | *Avocado Toast*

SERVES 4

Chileans have opinions. There are right and wrong ways to do things, especially when it comes to food. And even with something as simple as pan con palta, *you must toe the line or risk alienating Chilean guests. If you want to make authentic Chilean* pan con palta, *neither eggs nor cilantro nor anything out of the ordinary goes on top. Chileans will accept the following as toppings to this open-faced sandwich: a mild, short-aged cheese,* queso fresco *(in Chile, this is similar to Mexican* queso fresco, *but it is made with rennet), or ham.*

We use slightly firm Hass avocados, mashed (never sliced), and bakery bread. Unless you are preparing pan con palta *for a child, each person at the table builds their own, scooping the avocado with a fork, and using the back of the fork to spread it out.*

Like many of the recipes from the Once *section,* pan con palta *does double duty as a breakfast food. Avocado doesn't keep once mashed, so plan on eating all of what you mash. In our experience, this tends not to be a problem.*

4 slices of country loaf or 1
   baguette
2 avocados
1 teaspoon vegetable oil
Salt, to taste

1. Cut off the ends of the baguette. Slice the remaining piece in half and then split each of these down the middle.

2. Toast the open baguettes or sliced bread.

3. Scoop the avocado onto a plate and season with salt and 1 teaspoon of oil. Mash it well with a fork.

4. Spread the avocado on top of the bread.

5. Serve.

DOBLADITAS | *Folded Bread*

SERVES 10

Dobladitas *(literally: little folded things), made with a folded bread that looks a little like a clamshell, were born from having leftover empanada dough, though this recipe has a bit more baking powder to make them slightly lighter. The dough is pricked with a fork before baking, and it's one of few breads from Chile that has an egg wash. As they bake, they curl slightly, which makes their folds look a bit like a smile. There is no crumb to speak of, so crust-lovers, come close, your snack has arrived. The inner layers seem almost more steamed than baked, so while the outside is on the crunchy side, the inside is soft and moist.*

Speaking of the inside, that's the prize, because it's where the butter goes. We unfold them once, and spread with salted butter. Some people "stab" the surface so the butter sinks in better. Dobladitas are generally eaten straight from the oven, and though they began as a homemade solution to extra dough, they are now sold in bakeries as well, though then the race is on to get them home while they are still toasty warm and ready for a generous pat of butter.

3 cups all-purpose flour

1¼ teaspoons salt

1 tablespoon baking powder

4 tablespoons lard or unsalted butter, melted and warm

⅔ cup whole milk

1 egg, beaten

1. Preheat the oven to 400°F.

2. In a stand mixer bowl or food processor, combine the flour, salt, and baking powder.

3. With the machine running on low speed, add the lard or butter. Add the milk in a slow stream until a soft dough forms.

4. Place the dough on a floured counter and split into 10 equal pieces.

5. Roll each piece into 6½-inch circle, and fold in half into a half-moon, and then again into a quarter of a circle.

6. Place the *dobladitas* on a greased baking sheet or on top of parchment paper.

7. Brush with the egg and prick 3 times with a fork.

8. Bake for 20 minutes until golden. Serve hot.

LECHE CON FRUTILLAS | *Strawberry Smoothie*

SERVES 4

Forget about scooping artificially pink powder into a glass. This is not your childhood strawberry milk. This strawberry milk smoothie is a classic after-school snack for kids up to about middle school. In summer we might also make it with peaches or apricots, and in winter, leche con plátano (a banana smoothie) takes its place.

Although this treat is easily adapted, we have a special affinity for the version made with strawberries, perhaps because one of the original ancestors of the modern strawberry, the Fragaria chiloensis (often referred to as the white strawberry) originates in the south of Chile. It was taken out of Chile in the 1700s and later hybridized with one from Virginia to create the modern garden strawberry. Culinary patrimony aside, the modern red strawberry makes a flavorful treat and gives this beverage its distinctive pink hue.

1 pound strawberries
4 cups cold milk, whole or 2%
¼ cup honey (optional)

1. Wash and hull the strawberries.

2. Place the strawberries, milk, and optional honey in the blender and blend for 2 minutes.

3. Serve cold.

QUEQUE DE HIGOS | *Fig Bundt Cake*

SERVES 12

Much to the confusion of English speakers who study Spanish, in Chile, queque *does not mean a layer cake.* Queque *is fine-crumbed and sweet, and often baked in a Bundt pan. It makes a great snack, and if it takes a few days to eat it all (which we rather doubt), it keeps well, too.*

One big advantage of a queque *is that the batter is often made with oil, which doesn't have to be left out to soften like butter. Also, the batter is scoopably thick, so it holds the nuts and figs in suspension, distributing them throughout the* queque.

Fig trees have been cultivated for their fruit since at least 5000 BC, and in Chile, the combination of figs and walnuts is natural, as the trees grow well in the same kinds of conditions. Figs and walnuts are paired in calugas *(sweet confections somewhere between caramel and fudge) and several other desserts. The trees in Chile are the double-fruiting variety, which gives us plenty of both* brevas *(spring figs) and* higos *(late summer figs), which you can see drying on corrugated metal roofs in the countryside in Chile in season.*

½ cup whole milk
1 teaspoon lemon juice
3 eggs
1 cup granulated sugar
½ cup vegetable oil
2 cups all-purpose flour
1 teaspoon ground nutmeg
1 teaspoon ground cinnamon
½ teaspoon salt
1 teaspoon baking powder
1 cup chopped dried Mission
   figs, stems removed
1 cup chopped walnuts

1. Preheat the oven to 350°F.
2. Spray a Bundt cake pan with cooking spray.
3. Mix the milk with the lemon juice. It will curdle. Set it aside.
4. In a bowl, whisk the eggs until well mixed, about 30 seconds.
5. Add the sugar and oil. Mix well.
6. Add the flour, nutmeg, cinnamon, salt, and baking powder. Whisk a couple of times.
7. Add the milk and use a spatula to mix the batter.
8. Fold the figs and walnuts into the batter with a spatula.
9. Pour the batter in the pan and bake for 1 hour until golden and a cake tester inserted in the middle comes out clean.
10. Allow to cool on a cooling rack for 15 minutes before flipping it over to remove it from the pan.
11. Slice and serve.

SANDWICHES DE MIGA | *Finger Sandwiches*

SERVES 6

We make and serve these finger sandwiches—with the crusts cut off—for guests. It might be for a birthday—which in Chile is generally celebrated at home—or for a celebration after a baptism or other rite of passage, or if we are having guests over for once. *Here we include two recipes, one for a chicken–red pepper spread and one for a ham-and-cheese spread. Other popular variations include salami and cheese and* ave palta *(chicken avocado salad).*

If we have leftover filling, in Chile we scoop it into half of an avocado to serve as an appetizer or for a light lunch, or use it to make stuffed tomatoes or Betarragas Rellenas/Layered Stuffed Beets *(page 25). The sandwiches you can make a couple of hours ahead of time, and the spreads keep for a few days in the refrigerator. Wrap the ham spread tightly, because it oxidizes easily.*

AVE PIMENTÓN | *Chicken Salad with Roasted Red Peppers*

2 pounds bone-in chicken breast

¼ onion

1 carrot

A few pieces or sprigs of celery, parsley, or cilantro

Salt, to taste

Pepper, to taste

3 tablespoons mayonnaise

½ cup chopped roasted red peppers, drained

1 bag sliced sandwich bread, white or whole wheat

1. In a medium pot, place the chicken, onion, carrot, herbs, salt, and pepper. Cover with water. Cook over medium-high heat until boiling. Lower the heat to a simmer and scoop away and discard any foam. Cover and cook for 20 minutes.

2. Remove the chicken from the broth and let cool completely. Save the broth.

3. Remove the skin and bone from the chicken, and dice the meat small.

4. In a bowl, mix the chicken, mayonnaise, peppers, salt, and pepper. You want a soft paste, so add broth if necessary. Adjust the seasoning.

PASTA DE JAMÓN | *Ham Salad Spread*

½ pound cooked ham from the deli section

½ pound Havarti or Muenster cheese

3 tablespoons mayonnaise

Salt, to taste

Pepper, to taste

1 bag sliced sandwich bread, white or whole wheat

1. In a food processor, process the ham until it is almost a paste. Transfer it to a bowl.

2. Without rinsing the food processor bowl, process the cheese in the food processor until it forms granules. Add to the bowl with the ham.

3. Add the mayonnaise to the bowl. Mix well and taste. Adjust the seasoning.

TO ASSEMBLE THE SANDWICHES

1. Scoop 3 tablespoons of chicken or ham filling onto a slice of bread. Spread almost to the edge and cover with another slice. Refrigerate.

2. Just before serving, cut off the crusts of the bread and cut in half.

3. Wrap the sandwiches tightly so they don't brown.

PAN AMASADO | *Kneaded Bread*

MAKES 12

Pan amasado *is generally produced in small batches, made by individuals who sell it baked fresh, and it is entirely handmade.*

Along many roads in central Chile, you will see people shaking a white cloth at arm's distance, and that means that somewhere nearby, there is an horno de barro *(wood-fired clay oven) where someone is baking the next batch of empanadas or* pan amasado. *If you happen to be driving by, and you see the white cloth, you'd be a fool not to stop and pick up a dozen.*

The milk wash gives the bread a crisp crust, and the single rise yields uniform holes and a crumb that makes it resistant and springy. When it's hot, tear off pieces to spread with butter or top with Pebre/Chilean Salsa Fresca *(page 23) or* Salsa Verde/Parsley-Onion Salsa *(page 53). Larger* pan amasado *is used for sandwiches like the* Chacarero/Farmer's Steak Sandwich *(page 159). Bread is such an elemental food and so important in Chile that Gabriela Mistral, one of Chile's two Nobel Prize–winning poets, wrote the poem* Pan *in homage to it.*

1 teaspoon sugar
1 cup warm water
1 packet active dry yeast
4 cups all-purpose flour
1½ teaspoons salt
2 tablespoons melted
   butter
¼ cup milk, for brushing

1. Dissolve the sugar in the warm water and add the yeast. Mix and let rest for 10 minutes. It should be foamy.

2. In the bowl of a stand mixer set with the paddle attachment, add the flour and salt. Combine.

3. Add the butter and mix.

4. With the mixer running on slow, add the yeast and water. Work until a soft dough forms. If required, add more water 1 tablespoon at a time.

5. Switch to the dough hook and knead for 5 minutes.

6. Divide the dough into 12 equal portions, roll each one into a ball, and place them on a baking sheet. Cover with a kitchen towel and let them rise for 1 hour.

7. Preheat the oven to 350°F.

8. Brush each ball with milk and pierce the surface 3 times with a fork.

9. Bake for 30 minutes or until golden.

10. Serve warm.

CHACARERO | *Farmer's Steak Sandwich*

SERVES 4

You may think a sandwich is a sandwich. Stop saying that. Don't even think it within earshot of a Chilean talking about a chacarero, *one of the dishes that is the very embodiment of Chile's love affair with sandwiches.*

The name chacarero *makes reference to the* chacra *or vegetable garden that people in the country have at their homes. The garden-fresh tomatoes, hot pepper rounds, and green beans (yes, green beans!) that peek out from under the bread give it freshness and texture, and nothing of the expertly grilled meat is lost, with the bread used to soak up the juices left on the diner-style grill.*

So serious is our love for sandwiches that the person that works the grill in a fuente de soda—*the type of restaurant where they are served—has their own title, of* maestro sanguchero *(or* maestra sanguchera *in the case of a female sandwich master). They deftly manage the grill and build the* chacarero *so it can be picked up whole or in halves (though you may use cutlery if you prefer). No sauce is necessary for this succulent sandwich, and the tight crumb of the* pan amasado *somehow manages to contain the juicy tomatoes and meat perfectly.*

1 pound frozen green beans,
   French cut
1 large heirloom tomato
1 tablespoon vegetable oil
1 pound top sirloin, thinly sliced
Salt, to taste
Pepper, to taste
4 rustic hamburger buns or
   Pan Amasado/Kneaded Bread
   (page 157)
4 tablespoons mayonnaise
1 yellow Thai or sweet banana
   pepper, sliced in rounds,
   optional

1. Boil the green beans in salted water for 3 to 5 minutes. Drain and place them in a bowl with ice water.

2. Cut the tomato ¼-inch thick.

3. In a skillet, warm 1 tablespoon of oil over medium-high heat. Season the meat with salt and pepper. Cook 2 minutes each side.

4. Split the buns and lightly toast.

5. Drain the green beans and dress with salt and oil. Season the tomato.

6. Spread a thin layer of mayonnaise on the inside surfaces of each bun, put the meat on top of the base bun, add a tomato slice, and finish with the green beans. Add the optional peppers. Cover with the top of the bun.

7. Serve immediately.

COMPLETO | *Hot Dog*

SERVES 4

Many countries have their own distinctive way to serve a hot dog. The Chilean completo, *in almost complete disregard for a culture that generally looks down on handheld and potentially messy food, has a series of toppings that require a certain precision to allow you to get this all-ages treat to your mouth.*

Certainly, Chile owes some of its completo *culture to Germany, both for the hot dog sausage and the mandatory sauerkraut that adorns it. From there, the additions of avocado, mayonnaise, and tomato reflect the Chilean zeitgeist. Other permissible toppings (though here the name changes from* completo*) are* salsa americana *(similar to tartar sauce),* Salsa Verde/Parsley-Onion Salsa *(page 53), a spicy sauce called* pasta de ají, *and optional ketchup and a mild yellow mustard.*

Completos are a popular birthday party food, especially for children, but they fill almost every meal niche equally well (perhaps with the exception of breakfast), including the meal/snack we call the bajón, *which is the mid-partying middle of the night snack you eat to reanimate before continuing on. Buy bakery buns if you can, serve them warm, and boil, do not grill, the hot dogs for an authentic* completo *experience.*

4 hot dogs

2 avocados

2 tomatoes

Salt, to taste

4 hot dog buns

1 cup sauerkraut

4 tablespoons mayonnaise, and
   additional to serve

Ketchup, optional

Mustard, optional

1. To heat the hot dogs, put them in plenty of water and bring to a boil over medium-high heat. Lower the heat to a simmer.

2. Scoop out the avocadoes and mash. Season with salt.

3. Cut the tomatoes in small dice. Season with salt.

4. Toast the buns slightly or wrap in aluminum foil and warm up in the oven.

5. Open a bun and spread a thin layer of mayonnaise on the inside of both sides. Follow this with the hot dog, avocado, sauerkraut, and tomatoes and finish with mayonnaise, ketchup, and/or mustard.

6. Eat immediately.

ALFAJORES | *Dulce de Leche–Filled Sandwich Cookies*

MAKES 16

To know and love Chilean repostería *(sweet treats), is to embrace* manjar. *Everything from the* Torta Mil Hojas/*Dulce de Leche Thousand-Layer Cake (page 178), to* cachitos *(filled pastry "horns") can have* manjar *in it, and* manjar *is used to flavor ice cream and milk or simply spread on bread. But one of the quintessential ways to enjoy* manjar *is sandwiched between two thin round cookies, which we call an* alfajor.

The name alfajor *derives, like many Spanish words beginning with al-, from Arabic, and in many countries, it takes different forms. Here the cookie is sturdy and thin. Other versions may be filled with a dark sugary confection studded with walnuts, or use the less-commonly found* manjar blanco.

People don't often make alfajores *at home, but when they do, they generally buy* manjar *(or dulce de leche, as it is known in Argentina) from the supermarket. We're partial to the Chilean name* manjar, *a word also used to mean "nectar" in the expression el* manjar de las dioses *(nectar of the gods). They're a popular roadside snack in Chile, especially between Santiago and the coast.*

2 cups all-purpose flour
Pinch of salt
3 egg yolks
5 tablespoons whole milk
1 teaspoon apple cider vinegar
1 tablespoon unsalted butter, melted
1 (13.4-oz.) can dulce de leche
1 cup unsweetened shredded coconut

1. Place the flour and salt in a bowl. Mix.

2. Add the egg yolks and work with a fork until crumbs form.

3. Add the milk, vinegar, and butter. Keep working with the fork until the dough starts coming together. Knead by hand and add water by the teaspoon if needed. The resulting dough should be soft.

4. Knead for 10 minutes or until the dough feels elastic. Wrap in plastic wrap and refrigerate a minimum of 2 hours, or overnight.

5. Preheat the oven to 350°F.

6. Roll the dough out on a floured counter until it is very thin, almost translucent. Cut with a 3-inch round cutter. Lay on an unlined baking sheet. Prick each cookie 3 times with a fork.

7. Bake 12 minutes or until golden. Remove to a cooling rack.

8. Just before eating the cookies, spread one with a tablespoon or more of dulce de leche and press the other cookie on top until the dulce de leche comes close to the edge.

9. Spread a thin layer of dulce de leche around the rim of the cookie and then roll in coconut.

10. You can store the cookies, unfilled, in an airtight container for 10 days.

MENDOCINOS | *Shortbread-Style Sandwich Cookies*

MAKES 20

These cookies are next level from your standard alfajores, *a class of cookies Chile shares with Argentina and Peru. They have a complicated family tree, but have one thing in common: they sandwich a sweet filling between two cookies. In this case, the cookie is similar to a shortbread, buttery and firm, and you can just barely taste the addition of brown sugar. The top cookie is chocolate coated, and that adds an extra layer of luxury to this decadent cookie.*

People tend to buy mendocinos *at a bakery, and they're a snack you'd buy to eat on the way home from school or work. They occupy a similar place in the Chilean psyche as a donut might in the United States. Mendocino literally means "from Mendoza," a city just across the Andes from Santiago, but we've traveled to Mendoza, and discovered a whole other branch of the* alfajor *family tree, so let's just say that what's important here is that this cookie is delicious.*

8 tablespoons unsalted butter, room temperature

½ cup dark brown sugar

2 egg yolks

1 teaspoon vanilla extract

1¼ cups cornstarch

¾ cup all-purpose flour

1 (13.4-oz.) can dulce de leche

8 ounces semisweet chocolate baking wafers

1. In a stand mixer or with a hand mixer, beat the butter with the sugar until light and creamy, 3 minutes on high speed.

2. Add the egg yolks and vanilla and mix well.

3. Add the cornstarch and flour and mix at low speed until the dough starts to come together. It is like shortbread in that it will not come together completely in the mixer, and you must finish bringing together the dough by hand. Wrap in plastic wrap and refrigerate for at least 30 minutes or overnight.

4. Preheat the oven to 350°F. Cover a baking sheet with parchment paper.

5. Roll the dough on a floured surface to ¼-inch thickness. Cut 2 to 2½-inch circles, and place them on the baking sheet. They will not spread.

6. Bake for 13 to 15 minutes until their bottoms just brown. Let cool completely on the baking sheet.

7. Fill with 2 tablespoons of dulce de leche. Cover with another cookie.

8. Melt the chocolate wafers following the package instructions.

9. Place the filled cookies on a cooling rack with a tray under and pour chocolate over each cookie sandwich.

10. Allow to dry and serve at room temperature.

KUCHEN DE MORA | *Blackberry Cream Tart*

SERVES 8

Chile owes its love of kuchen—a fruit-based confection—to the historical German presence in the country. There were multiple waves of state-sponsored immigration, as early as the 1840s, mainly to the Lakes Region, about ten hours south of Santiago. That's also where the strongest culture of kuchen making and eating is centered in Chile.

Kuchen (the ch is an aspirated h sound like the ch- in Chanukah) is a highly seasonal dish, based on whatever fruit is ripest and most readily available. In summer, that's often berries, and this blackberry kuchen has a dough that's somewhere between the texture of a cookie and a cake, both before and after baking. It crumbles, but it's not greasy, and it slices beautifully. The custardy topping is a bit like the filling of a southern buttermilk pie, and it sinks into all the nooks and crannies around the berries.

When berries go out of season, the kuchen recipe changes a bit, and apples take over as the filling. There's even a walnut version that is not entirely dissimilar to pecan pie. Kuchen might sound like a special-occasion treat to you, but the fruit versions really aren't overly sweet, and in the south of Chile, kuchen nearly always graces the once *table.*

For the dough

4 tablespoons unsalted butter, room temperature
1 cup granulated sugar, divided
1 egg
1 teaspoon vanilla extract
¾ cup all-purpose flour
1 teaspoon baking powder

For the filling

¼ cup cornstarch
2 cups cold whole milk
1 (3-inch) cinnamon stick
2 cups blackberries
1 tablespoon powdered sugar, to serve, optional

1. **Make the dough:** Preheat the oven to 375°F.

2. Grease a 14x6-inch rectangular or 8-inch round springform tart pan with butter.

3. In a bowl, mix the butter and ½ cup of sugar with a fork.

4. Add the egg and the vanilla and mix well.

5. Add the flour with the baking powder and form a soft dough.

6. Move the dough to the tart pan and, using wet fingertips, press the dough all around to cover the base completely.

7. Bake for 20 minutes or until golden brown.

8. **Make the filling:** Dissolve the cornstarch in the cold milk, add the remaining ½ cup of sugar and cinnamon, and cook over medium heat until it comes to a boil. Stir frequently, especially as it begins to thicken. Allow it to boil gently for 1 minute, stirring continuously.

9. Place the blackberries on top of the baked base.

10. Place the tart pan on top of a baking sheet.

11. Pour the hot filling over the blackberries and smooth the top.

12. Bake for 20 minutes or until the top is golden. It will bubble up in the oven.

13. Turn the oven off, open the door a crack, and allow the kuchen to cool there for 15 minutes.

14. Serve at room temperature or cold. Keep refrigerated and dust with powdered sugar before serving.

PAN DE HUEVO | *Sweet Egg Bread Rolls*
MAKES 8

On the beaches on the central coast of Chile, it's not uncommon to hear someone, usually a man wearing a long white button-front overshirt, walking down the beach calling out "pan de huevo" selling this mildly sweet, vanilla-flavored egg bread, from a wide wicker basket. It's a popular snack, made all the more special by the warm sunshine and fresh air of being at the beach.

Pan de huevo is easy to make at home, and it requires no rise time as it's made with baking powder. It is a dense, stiff bread, with a dry, tight crumb. You might liken it to somewhere between a scone and bread, and it's delicious warm, spread with butter.

2 cups all-purpose flour
1 tablespoon baking powder
½ cup powdered sugar
Pinch of salt
3 eggs, divided
1 teaspoon vanilla extract
3 tablespoons unsalted butter,
    melted and cooled

1. Preheat the oven to 350°F.

2. Mix the flour, baking powder, sugar, and salt in a medium bowl.

3. In a small bowl, beat together two eggs, vanilla, and butter until well mixed.

4. Pour over the dry ingredients and mix at first with a fork and then with your hands. If needed, add 1 teaspoon of water at a time to form a soft dough.

5. Knead the dough for 5 minutes. Split the dough in 8 equal portions on a floured counter. Roll into balls and then flatten them slightly with your palm.

6. Score an x on top of each roll.

7. Beat the remaining egg and brush it on top.

8. Bake for 20 to 25 minutes or until golden.

MIEL DE MELÓN | *Honeydew Melon Syrup*

MAKES 3 CUPS

Though we love the freshness of this surprising syrup made from honeydew, it is so old school that many Chileans of today may only vaguely remember it. It's a great way to recapture the simple summer flavor of ripe fruit when it is no longer in season, and melon more readily lends itself to syrup than to jam.

This recipe makes a syrup reminiscent of honey that can be drizzled on desserts such as Suspiro de Monja/Fried Choux Pastry (page 71), or be used in place of any other syrup. We also suspect it would work in mixed drinks, but haven't yet had the chance to try, so if you do, please let us know how it goes.

Chilean lore dictates that you not try to make this or any syrup at night as it will never reach the right viscosity. You can try, but don't say we didn't warn you. Also, during cooking, the syrup recipe bubbles up quite a bit, so use a tall pot, and keep an eye on it.

1 large ripe honeydew melon
   (about 3 pounds)
¼ cup water
Granulated sugar
1 tablespoon lemon juice

1. Split the melon and remove the seeds. Scoop the melon out of the rind and cut the flesh into large cubes.

2. In a pot, add ¼ cup of water and the melon cubes, and cook covered for 20 to 30 minutes, or until the pulp is soft.

3. Strain through a cheesecloth, without squeezing. Discard the melon.
Measure the liquid and pour into a pot.

4. Add 1 cup of sugar for each cup of liquid.

5. Cook for 30 to 45 minutes on a gentle simmer, or until syrupy and golden in color, stirring frequently.

6. Add the lemon juice and mix well.

7. Keep at room temperature.

CAFÉ HELADO | *Coffee Ice Cream Float*

SERVES 4

It may be hard to imagine, but there are particular cafés in Chile that are known specifically for their café helado, *or coffee ice cream floats. Children in Chile taste coffee from a very young age, and it's considered as basic a flavor as chocolate or vanilla. People often go to a café to order this celebratory drink for the end of the school year or just for a late-afternoon snack.*

   Café helado is often served in a tall glass and always both with a spoon and a straw, so you can drink first, and eat later. Garnishes may include a rolled cookie or a maraschino cherry, and while traditionalists insist on vanilla ice cream, people have been known to branch out.

   Unlike a milkshake, this drink is only mildly sweet, and you would never, ever order it to go. Café helados are meant for long conversation and maybe a plate of cookies or a slice or two of kuchen for the table. And while someone might ask for a bite of your ice cream, it is understood that your café helado *is yours alone.*

1 cup cold heavy whipping cream
2 tablespoons granulated sugar, divided
2 cups cold milk
2 espresso shots, or 2 tablespoons instant coffee dissolved in ¼ cup hot water
1 cup French vanilla ice cream

1. Whip the cream until soft peaks form, then add 1 tablespoon of sugar, and keep whipping until hard peaks form. Keep cold.

2. Remove the ice cream from the freezer to temper it slightly.

3. Combine the cold milk, remaining 1 tablespoon of sugar, and coffee.

4. In each glass, place a generous scoop of vanilla ice cream. Add the coffee milk until about 1 inch under the rim.

5. Add the whipped cream.

6. Serve immediately with a spoon and a straw.

BRAZO DE REINA | *Dulce de Leche Swiss Roll*

SERVES 8

This well-loved, old-school Chilean dessert is made like a Swiss roll, which allegedly resembles the arm of a queen (for which it is named) before it is sliced. It's good for a special once, like one on a Sunday, or when you've got guests. In Chile, it's sold in bakeries, beside meringues, berlines (filled donuts), and other single-serve sweets, usually laid out in fluted waxed paper cups.

While the traditional filling for the brazo de reina *is manjar, we'd recommend swapping in* Dulce de Camote/Sweet Potato Butter *(page 139) for a surprisingly colorful and different spin. We have heard, but cannot corroborate, that there are some people in the world who think that not every dessert needs to have manjar. One advantage of using the* Dulce de Camote *is that even your friends who are dairy-free can eat it.*

The ends of the Brazo de Reina *are not the prettiest part, and they seldom make it out of the kitchen, a reward for the chef or whatever lucky household member happens to walk by.*

4 eggs, separated
⅓ cup granulated sugar
⅓ cup packed dark brown sugar
4 tablespoons vegetable oil
1 teaspoon vanilla extract
¾ cup all-purpose flour, sifted
1 teaspoon baking powder
¼ teaspoon salt
1 (13.4-oz.) can dulce de leche, room temperature
2 tablespoons powdered sugar
½ cup shredded coconut

1. Preheat the oven to 325°F. Grease and cover a rimmed baking sheet with parchment paper.

2. In a bowl, with a hand or stand mixer, whisk the egg whites and the granulated sugar together until hard peaks form.

3. In another bowl, whisk the egg yolks, dark brown sugar, oil, and vanilla until pale, about 3 minutes.

4. Add the flour, baking powder, and salt to the egg yolk mix. Whisk until just combined.

5. With a spatula, fold the egg whites into the batter.

6. Spread the batter flat on the baking sheet, to a ½-inch thickness.

7. Bake for 15 to 18 minutes, until golden.

8. Dust a kitchen towel with the powdered sugar. Remove the cake from the oven and flip it onto the towel, remove the baking sheet, and peel off the parchment paper. Gently roll the cake together with the towel, starting with the short end. Be careful not to break the cake. Let cool for an hour.

9. Gently unroll and fill with a thick ¼-inch layer of dulce de leche. Reroll and pat the coconut onto the outside of the cake.

10. Serve in ½-inch slices at room temperature.

TORTA DE PANQUEQUE CHOCOLATE FRAMBUESA | *Raspberry Chocolate "Crepe" Cake*

SERVES 18

Chileans love cake, and it's not unusual or rude to ask, if you know cake will be served (as on a birthday), to find out what kind, to see if you should save room. Though chocolate is not nearly as popular in Chile as in the United States, like everywhere, we have our chocolate-lovers, and the contrast of the tart raspberry with the dark chocolate is legendary. Other traditional fillings for this cake would include lúcuma-manjar, *and a sweet custard called* huevo mol. *Try lemon curd, or any other spreadable filling with this versatile multi-layered cake.*

We call this a "crepe" cake, though the batter is thick enough to spread, as opposed to pour. Traditionalists would make this in the oven, but this method is quicker and less prone to burning, and the results are indistinguishable.

Most families in Chile would order, as opposed to make, this cake, but either way we'd serve it in narrow slices, because it's quite rich. But not so rich that Chileans won't engage in the time-old tradition of having a slice of their leftover birthday cake for breakfast the next day.

For the ganache

8 ounces semi-dark chocolate

1 cup heavy whipping cream

1 cup unsalted butter, room temperature, divided

For the batter

1 cup granulated sugar

10 eggs, separated

1¼ cups all-purpose flour, sifted

1 (13-oz.) jar raspberry jam

1. **Prepare the ganache:** Chop the chocolate in small pieces.

2. Bring the cream to a simmer on a small pot. Pour it over the chocolate and wait 1 minute.

3. Using a spatula, gently and without lifting the spatula from the bottom of the pot, mix the chocolate completely.

4. Add 2 tablespoons of butter and mix in well. Set aside; don't refrigerate.

5. **Prepare the batter:** In the bowl of the stand mixer, using the whisk attachment, cream the remaining butter with the sugar until very smooth, 5 minutes. Add the egg yolks one by one, mixing in each one completely before adding the next.

6. In another bowl, whisk the egg whites to hard peaks.

7. Fold the egg whites into the batter.

8. Add the flour and gently mix in.

9. Warm a 10-inch nonstick skillet, scoop out ½ cup of the batter, and using an offset spatula, smooth the surface. Cook for 2 minutes, until cooked through, and barely brown.

10. Place on a serving plate and spread with 2 tablespoons of ganache.

11. Repeat with the rest of the batter. Alternate the ganache and the raspberry jam as filling.

12. Cover with any remaining ganache or leave bare.

TORTA MIL HOJAS
Dulce de Leche Thousand-Layer Cake
SERVES 30

There's no way around the fact that this highly esteemed cake is an undertaking, but the result is so impressive that we think you should make it anyway. It has been made in Chile for generations, and unlike cakes with cream or fresh fruit, does not require refrigeration. It's unusual for someone to share their recipe for this cake, and this one has been in Pilar's family for generations.

Torta Mil Hojas is served for birthdays, Christmas, or other celebratory events. It is never eaten on the same day it's made, to give time for the dulce de leche and contrasting marmalade (here we have it with sour cherry, but plum or raspberry work as well) to soak in a bit to the crisp layers. The name "thousand layer" may seem a bit of an exaggeration, but each one of the 14 to 16 layers puffs into several and we tend to lose count.

Torta mil hojas keeps for about 5 days. But it's unlikely to make it that long.

3¼ cups all-purpose flour

¼ teaspoon salt

1 cup butter, diced and room temperature

3 egg yolks

¾ cup whole milk

1 tablespoon rum or pisco

2 (13.4-oz.) cans dulce de leche

2½ cups finely chopped walnuts

1 (14-oz.) jar black cherry jam

¼ cup powdered sugar

1. In a bowl, whisk the flour and salt together. With the stand or hand mixer working on low speed add the butter, yolks, milk, and rum or pisco. Stop as soon as a soft dough forms. Wrap the dough in plastic wrap, flatten into a disc, and refrigerate overnight.

2. Preheat the oven to 350°F. Prepare a 9-inch parchment paper circle as a template.

3. Cut the disc of dough into 12 equal parts, and keep one out to work with, returning the rest to the fridge. Roll the dough out onto parchment paper, into a round large enough to cut a 9-inch circle out of it. Carefully transfer the parchment paper with the dough circle to a baking sheet. Prick with a fork several times.

4. Bake for 5 to 7 minutes, until golden. Let cool on a rack, and repeat with the 11 remaining pieces of dough.

5. Reroll your leftovers, and bake as before.

6. Choose the least attractive of your baked circles and set it aside.

7. Spread the first circle with 4 tablespoons of dulce de leche, cover with another disk, and spread the same amount of dulce de leche and 2 tablespoons of chopped walnuts. On top of the following disk, spread 4 tablespoons of jam. Repeat until done with all layers other than the one you set aside.

8. Break the reserved circle into small pieces and mix with the remaining walnuts and powdered sugar.

9. Use a butter knife to spread the whole cake with a thin layer of dulce de leche. Press the mixture of walnuts, crumbled pastry, and powdered sugar into the dulce de leche on top and on the sides.

10. Refrigerate overnight. Serve at room temperature.

COLA DE MONO | *Coffee Eggnog*

SERVES 8

This is Chile's version of a milky alcoholic beverage served from Christmas to New Year's. You may liken it to the (somewhat different) coquito of the Caribbean, or perhaps even eggnog in your own home. Though it is fabulously popular, we really only drink it at Christmas time, and more often than not, it is paired with Pan de Pascua/Christmas Cake (page 182). It's available prepared commercially, but the best cola de mono (which literally means monkey's tail) is always made at home. In many friend groups or families there's one recipe that is considered the best, and it's not unusual to bring a bottle of this homemade drink to a friend's house, often in a recycled pisco bottle. It's considered a nice gift.

You might think of it as a coffee cream liqueur, but without the thickeners. It's served in a juice glass, generally without ice. It's sweet, but because it contains distilled alcohol, it still packs quite a punch.

3 cups whole milk
1 (14-oz.) can condensed milk
3 whole cloves
1 (3-inch) cinnamon stick
½ teaspoon ground nutmeg
4 tablespoons instant
   Colombian coffee
1 cup pisco, grappa, or vodka

1. In a medium pot, combine the milk, condensed milk, spices, and coffee

2. Bring to a boil over medium heat, and let simmer 5 minutes. Let cool.

3. Strain and discard the spices. Add the pisco, grappa, or vodka. Taste and add more alcohol if desired.

4. Serve cold. Keep refrigerated for up to a week.

PAN DE PASCUA | *Sweet Christmas Bread*
SERVES 8

The word Pascua *is used to refer to Easter, but in Chile we use the expression* Felices Pascuas *to mean Merry Christmas. As in many countries, Chile has many specific foods eaten at this time of the year, and* Pan de Pascua *is popular among people of all belief systems. Far more relevant at this time of year than your religious affiliation is where you stand on the inclusion of candied fruit in this spiced cake.*

Every family has a different recipe, and this one—which includes manjar *and peanuts—has a moister crumb than many other versions we've tried.* Pan de Pascua *can be expensive to make, and in leaner years, families may fold in less fruit and fewer nuts. Chileans consider this a* queque, *even though it is called a bread, much like banana bread is not really bread either. The natural accompaniment to this cake is* Cola de Mono/Coffee Eggnog *(page 181), and the cake is eaten out of hand in the office, at school events, or anywhere you go between about Christmas and New Year's.* Pan de Pascua *could theoretically last ten days, but we have never seen one stick around that long.*

½ cup golden raisins
½ cup chopped walnuts
½ cup almonds
½ cup unsalted roasted peanuts
1 cup candied fruit, minced
½ teaspoon ground cinnamon
½ teaspoon ground nutmeg
½ teaspoon ground cloves
Zest of 1 lemon
2 tablespoons rum
8 tablespoons unsalted butter,
    room temperature
1 cup powdered sugar
2 eggs
1 cup dulce de leche
2½ cups all-purpose flour
1 teaspoon baking powder
Pinch of salt

1. Mix the raisins, walnuts, almonds, peanuts, candied fruit, spices, and lemon in a bowl. Add the rum. Mix well and cover with plastic wrap, and let the fruit and nuts sit overnight with the alcohol.

2. Preheat the oven to 300°F. Cover the bottom of an 8-inch cake pan with parchment paper and grease the sides.

3. Whip the butter with the sugar until light and creamy, about 5 minutes.

4. Add the eggs, one by one, mixing 1 minute after each addition.

5. Add the dulce de leche and mix well, about 3 minutes.

6. Add the flour, baking powder, and salt, and mix just enough to blend.

7. Add the nuts, fruit, and spices, and use a spatula to fold them into the batter.

8. Pour into the cake pan and smooth the top.

9. Bake for 1 to 1½ hours or until golden and a stick inserted in the middle comes out clean.

10. Let cool on a cooling rack 20 minutes. Unmold and let cool completely.

11. Serve room temperature. Stores well wrapped for up to 10 days.

Acknowledgments

First of all, we would like to thank the home cooks of Chile who have passed down their recipes for generations and kept families well fed in every kind of weather and in the face of great challenges. We are so thankful for our connection with Chile; its rich history, fertile land, and plentiful, fresh ingredients, and the patterns of immigration have allowed our food traditions to develop exactly how they have.

Then we would like to thank Houston, home to Pilar and her family. Her home there proved to be a great place to take photos, in natural light, providing us with stable weather in a city that cannot always depend on clear skies (to put it mildly). And also in Houston are the small-and-not-so-small fruit, vegetable, fish, and meat vendors who supplied us so seamlessly with the freshest, top-quality ingredients we used for the cookbook. A special shout-out to José from Airline Seafood, who packed up the salmon and barely laughed when we said we'd walk him home in his box of ice. And to Law Ranch for the Spanish chorizo, and Central Market where they sell Chilean raisins and olives from the

Azapa Valley, just like in Chile. And to the many vendors at the Urban Harvest Farmers Market, where we sourced fresh vegetables, bread, herbs, and flowers, and where Pilar has volunteered for many years.

We are thankful to the multiple agents that responded favorably to our proposal, and we were sorry we couldn't work with all of you. We are thankful to Ashley Collom, who skillfully guided us to rewrite our proposal and change the project a bit to make it more appealing to publishers, and who negotiated our contract and sold our book. We are also thankful to Meg Thompson for stepping in to finish up the book with us, and for supporting us through this process. We are thankful to the two agencies, first DeFiore and Company and then Thompson Literary Agency, who took a chance on a cookbook from a long, skinny country many people could not place on a map.

To our editor, Leah, we are thankful for her excitement about our project, her careful eye, and openness to the occasional semi-unexpected office visit. We are thankful to our designer Daniel

Brount and everyone who helped put together this book as we envisioned it. We also thank our publisher, Skyhorse, for believing in our tribute to Chile and the food that helps feed this nation we have both called home.

We are thankful to Araceli Paz, our rockstar Chilean food photographer, who shared our vision of this cookbook and shared her ideas about art and food in the shooting process. You are a master with natural light and food styling, and we will forever think of you when making tall food.

Pilar is thankful to her husband and children, who understand that the kitchen is her laboratory and command center and respect her space and her need for things to be just so. She also thanks the three of them for listening to all of her stories and celebrating her successes.

She also thanks Micky and Jackie for hosting her family during the cooking and shooting process so we could focus all of our attention on the cookbook. She thanks her Houston friends, who have always supported her efforts, for their curiosity and interest in discovering Chilean food.

She thanks her mother, her grandmother, her great-aunts, her aunts, and their friends, for feeding her with love. For sharing the recipes and stories of her family, and for raising her with respect for Chilean food, its ingredients, and the people involved in its cultivation, care, and preparation.

Pilar also thanks the readers of her original Spanish-language blog, *En Mi Cocina Hoy* (www.enmicocinahoy. com), who have been cooking with her since 2008 and who have been a great sounding board to solve hotly contested food debates, such as whether or not fruit is still dried on metal roofs in the countryside.

Eileen is thankful for her parents' interest in trying foods from many different places, and the "Gourmet Club" they had with friends that brought food from different worlds into hers. She is also thankful to her grandfather for teaching her to go far and wide to different specialty markets to get the food that makes your heart sing.

She is thankful to the many editors she has worked with over the years, who have encouraged her writing and her voice, and especially to Marie Elena Martinez, first at *Latin Kitchen* and then at *New Worlder*, for working with her on some early pieces on Chilean food and flavors. She is also thankful to Maria

Godoy at NPR's *The Salt* for commissioning the story that made her reach out to Pilar and get the ball rolling on this project and also for her enthusiasm about *The Chilean Kitchen*.

Eileen is also thankful to her many Chilean friends for encouraging her to explore Chilean food and sharing their food memories, stories, and sayings, and to faraway friends who offer continued understanding of the freelance life. She is also thankful to Pilar's family, who willingly gave up their mother, wife, living room, kitchen, and even bedrooms (thanks, Julia!) so that we could create this cookbook in a tiny piece of the most concentrated *chilenidad* Houston may ever have seen.

This book could not have happened without each of us having moved to each other's country. We are thankful for the processes and choices that each of us made to lead us to where we ended up, for our own curiosity that made us discover one another, and to networking technology, most notably WhatsApp and file-sharing platforms that allowed us to work on this cookbook with many thousands of miles between us. And for trusting each other to work together for more than a year before ever even meeting in person, which we may or may not have failed to mention in the original proposal.

Finally, we are thankful to each and every one of you who picks up this book and makes a special meal for friends and family. Likewise, those of you who regard the photos in this book as the artwork that they are also deserve our thanks. Lastly, for all of you who have picked up this book, who have tried these recipes, or who might now think differently or more proudly about your own traditional foods, we are also eternally grateful.

Index

Conversion Charts

METRIC AND IMPERIAL CONVERSIONS
(These conversions are rounded for convenience)

Ingredient	Cups/Tablespoons/Teaspoons	Ounces	Grams/Milliliters
Butter	1 cup/ 16 tablespoons/ 2 sticks	8 ounces	230 grams
Cheese, shredded	1 cup	4 ounces	110 grams
Cream cheese	1 tablespoon	0.5 ounce	14.5 grams
Cornstarch	1 tablespoon	0.3 ounce	8 grams
Flour, all-purpose	1 cup/1 tablespoon	4.5 ounces/0.3 ounce	125 grams/8 grams
Flour, whole wheat	1 cup	4 ounces	120 grams
Fruit, dried	1 cup	4 ounces	120 grams
Fruits or veggies, chopped	1 cup	5 to 7 ounces	145 to 200 grams
Fruits or veggies, pureed	1 cup	8.5 ounces	245 grams
Honey, maple syrup, or corn syrup	1 tablespoon	0.75 ounce	20 grams
Liquids: cream, milk, water, or juice	1 cup	8 fluid ounces	240 milliliters
Oats	1 cup	5.5 ounces	150 grams
Salt	1 teaspoon	0.2 ounce	6 grams
Spices: cinnamon, cloves, ginger, or nutmeg (ground)	1 teaspoon	0.2 ounce	5 milliliters
Sugar, brown, firmly packed	1 cup	7 ounces	200 grams
Sugar, white	1 cup/1 tablespoon	7 ounces/0.5 ounce	200 grams/12.5 grams
Vanilla extract	1 teaspoon	0.2 ounce	4 grams

OVEN TEMPERATURES

Fahrenheit	Celsius	Gas Mark
225°	110°	¼
250°	120°	½
275°	140°	1
300°	150°	2
325°	160°	3
350°	180°	4
375°	190°	5
400°	200°	6
425°	220°	7
450°	230°	8